You,

_____ *Rosemary* _____,

can positively impact the future by remembering the following:

If you want to touch the past, pick up a rock.
If you want to touch the present, smell a rose.
If you want to touch the future, touch a child.

God's Blessings,

_____
Bob Alexander

15.   *Philippians 4:8*

The Teacher Trap

THE

And How I CAN

TEACHER

Break Free

TRAP

by Bob Alexander

THE ALEXANDER RESOURCE GROUP | MACON, GA

ISBN: 0-9718829-0-8

The Alexander Resource Group
176 Lake View Drive North
Macon, Georgia 31210
1-877-872-4226
© 2002 Bob Alexander
All rights reserved.
Printed in the United States of America

Bob Alexander

The paper used in this publication meets the minimum requirements
of American National Standard for Information Sciences—
Permanence of Paper for Printed Library Materials.

CIP Information on file with the Library of Congress

praise for

The Teacher Trap

"*The Teacher Trap* is the right book at the right time. It should be required reading for educators, parents and other stakeholders in the care and rearing of the next generation. Mr. Alexander is to be commended for authoring this thought provoking and timely book about how to face the latest challenge facing public education."

—Earl Lennard Ph.D.
Superintendent, School District of Hillsborough County

•

"*The Teacher Trap* is the antidote for curing the ills of education. Bob Alexander has taken the 'wisdom of the ages' and given students, teachers and parents a solid foundation for reaching the pathway to prosperity. I highly recommend this book."

—Joe Miller
Three Rivers STW and Tech Prep Consortium

"*The Teacher Trap* is a concise, to the point roadmap for building character in the youth of America. Bob's book straight forwardly addresses problems and offers solutions on how to 'raise the bar' in education. A must-read."

—Judy Godfrey
Director, Staff Development, Bibb County Schools

•

"I've seen Bob and his programs work successfully in my schools before so I'm not surprised by *The Teacher Trap* at all. He concisely outlines the problems confronting education today with energy and offers his solutions with sincerity and integrity. I'll proudly keep it right next to his last book *Making It Happen*."

—Keith Cowne
Superintendent, Madison County Schools

•

"*The Teacher Trap* has identified a major problem in society today—students entering our schools lacking positive character traits. Bob's three basic qualities of Honesty, Accepting Responsibility and Respect for others are key characteristics that each child needs to possess in order to succeed in life. Who else can better tell this story than Bob Alexander? As a former educator he has experienced the world of teaching kids and the problems that are within the educational system. His book identifies the challenges and offers solutions. Educators, parents and decision-makers should read this book. They will be glad they did.

—G. David Carpenter
National Distinguished Principal – 1999
Eagle Springs Elementary

"For years I have witnessed the amazing effects your presentations have had on our students and faculty. Since implementing the I CAN Character Curriculum, our results have been incredible. *The Teacher Trap* provides real life solutions to an unreal society. An absolute must read!

—Angela T. Rasmussen, DDS
Gentle Dentistry

•

" *The Teacher Trap* clearly describes the problems facing teachers today and offers the I CAN Program as the solution. We have used this program effectively for four years—AND IT WORKS! Anyone interested in correcting the downward spiral of character development in children should read this book."

—Joe Corley
9th Degree Black Belt, Black Belt Hall of Fame

•

"A trap has been described as something easy to get into and hard to get out of. In *The Teacher Trap* Bob Alexander 'opens the door' by providing a simple blueprint for constructive change by focusing on the development of essential character traits. This book is not only timely, its principles are timeless."

—Dr. Terry W. Alderman
Author and Education consultant

•

"As long as there is hope, anything is possible. That is what *The Teacher Trap* re-creates in my heart...hope. The frustrations present day educators experience is validated in Bob's book.

He honors the hard work teachers put forth and examines the stance of values in our society. He also regenerates hope for what educators can do for students, families and communities. As I read the book, I found my hope for humanity rejuvenated, my passion as a school administrator re-ignited, and my spirit saying, 'Yes, I CAN' make a difference in the lives of others. Highly recommended reading!"

—Phyllis J. Rouse,
Principal, Yulee Elementary School

•

"My daughter is a first year teacher and Bob Alexander's book, *The Teacher Trap,* has the answers for many of the problems and frustrations that she has encountered. I will highly recommend the book to her and all educators and parents who want to positively impact the life of a child.

—Bobby Pope
Athletic Director, Mercer University

•

"Working in small, rural, economically disadvantaged schools for over 20 years, I continue to hear more frustrations of concerns from teachers that refer to character issues than from low pay or state and federal mandates. *The Teacher Trap* exemplifies the I CAN attitude of Bob Alexander in helping schools provide a foundation for success for its young people."

—Keith Shoulders
Superintendent, Providence City Schools

"As an educational leader, public speaker and author, Bob Alexander has 'been there, done that and has the tee shirt.' *The Teacher Trap* brings into focus all of his experiences and expresses the belief that character education is also a responsibility of the schools. Bob reminds us that from its beginning, public education has done more than teach the '3 R's.' There has always been, and will continue to be, a role of passing along to upcoming generations the fundamental beliefs necessary for society to function."

—Dr. Jim Puckett, Executive Director
Georgia Association of Educational Leaders

•

"Shortly after becoming the Head Football Coach at the University of Miami, I knew our program needed an infusion of passion and enthusiasm, coupled with a message intended to develop character and leadership. We invited Bob to address our entire football program—players, coaches and support personnel. It was a smashing success! The ideas he presented lit a fire and inspired us all. *The Teacher Trap* captures the critical ideas and philosophies so important to building relationships with young people of all ages, and are the true building blocks of success."

—Butch Davis
NFL Head Football Coach, Cleveland Browns

"*The Teacher Trap* is a quality book by a quality person. Bob Alexander has helped me with chapel programs for professional athletes for several years, and has NEVER disappointed the athletes or me. He is competent, capable and bleeds character. He takes the important information of education, explains the valuable concepts and helps apply it. My friend, Bob Alexander, is one of the best! I recommend him highly."

—John A. Weber
Athletes in Action

•

"As an educator for over 30 years, I have seen a lot of different things come and go. Of all the books I have read, *The Teacher Trap* is one of the most practical and to the point readings I have ever experienced. It addresses the problems and offers solutions on how to help educators make a difference in the lives of children."

—Henry L. Cooper
Director, Middle Georgia RESA

•

"*The Teacher Trap* provides statistical proof that teaching character traits of honesty, accepting responsibility and respecting others gives kids a better opportunity for success in life. You cannot go wrong with this excellent book."

—Terry Boehm
President, Pinellas County Education Foundation

To my parents, James and Juanita Alexander,
the greatest teachers of them all.

To my wife Pattie, whose love, kindness and
patience has inspired hundreds of students.

To our four children, Britton, Brad, Ashley
and Stephanie. Your love, laughter, and
daily lessons in life continue to bless me.

*Train up a child in the way he
should go: and when he is old
he will not depart from it.*

Proverbs 22:6

contents

The ultimate goal of American education is to produce educated human beings, capable of being responsible for themselves and productive in a competitive economy. The crisis is that children must be educated now and prepared to take their place in a competitive world. The future of our nation and the world depends on it.

The parents of American school children are frustrated with the educational problems in the public schools and want some significant improvements. There are many concerned parents who take an active role in the education of their children. Unfortunately, there are far more who don't. The number one problem of most teachers is related to the parents of the children they are trying to teach.

Thousands who became teachers found themselves mired in an educational nightmare that crushed their original dreams. Many teachers are tempted to quit the profession, but most of them keep on teaching in spite of the difficulty and the frustration they face every day in their classrooms. Statistics reveal there is a major problem in our schools regarding the character of the children. Teachers are on the front line of addressing this issue.

Honesty is the character quality that forms the foundational bedrock of every human being. Our greatest distortions of truth involve our impulsive reactions to the behavior of other people. Another facet of honesty involves what we have done in the past, what we are doing in the present, and what we will do in the future. Human deception is not new. People have been telling lies about themselves and others for as long as history has recorded human behavior. Children need to understand the full effect the issue of honesty will have upon their entire lives.

We have become a nation populated by large numbers of people who do not want to accept responsibility for their own actions. One of the main concerns of teachers and administrators is that they will be sued by the parents of the children they are trying to teach. When people can accept their roles in failure or disappointment or for problem behaviors (excessive alcohol use, taking drugs, dishonesty, etc.), they have the ability to overcome those problems and improve their future.

The principle of respect is foundational to the American experience because we are a nation of laws. A lack of respect for the law begins with a lack of respect for other concepts and principles. There are three major categories of respect that must be understood. The three categories are: Respect for Authority, Respect for Property, and Respect for Self and Others.

What are the desired results of character education? Whose values should be taught and how should principles of character be presented? The goal of character education should be to prepare students to be more successful in life! Successful people have to know how to read and write and they also need to understand how honesty, accepting responsibility, and showing respect for others will impact their future.

When students are taught the principles of character discussed in this book, their academic and personal lives are tremendously enhanced. Students enrolled in the I CAN program learn how to identify and obtain what they want in life through a plan of action. Time and time again, test and survey results show that students who adopt the traits of honesty, respect, and responsibility excel.

I have had a deep interest in the education of young people my entire life. I have always believed that education goes beyond the "3 R's." By far the most important information I learned in my life came from the influence of my mother and several special individuals, many of them teachers, who touched my life as I was growing up in Yazoo City, Mississippi.

Bob Alexander's book, *The Teacher Trap,* is the kind of book that is specifically written for times such as these by a man who knows first hand the pressures that our children, teachers, and school leaders are facing today. He knows because he has walked in their shoes. Bob is a former teacher, coach, and high school administrator who has a heart for children and professional teachers. As Director of Educational Services with our company, he traveled across America teaching students, teachers, and principals how to reach their full potential through the proven principles of the I CAN way of life. He knows first hand that we will never teach the ABC's of education until we teach the ABC's of life: Attitude, Behavior and Character.

The Teacher Trap captures ideas and concepts that hold the key to not only building character in our children, but to strengthening the fabric of our nation. I am particularly supportive of the three basic qualities Bob believes form the foundation of character-based education: Honesty, Accepting Responsibility, and Respect for Others. These are the same qualities that my mother taught me and I have tried to live by all my life. Our word should be, must be, our bond. We must accept responsibility for our own success and failure and we must value the lives of others by being willing to help them along life's path.

If you've been wondering what you can do to turn the world of education in the right direction, I believe that the ideas Bob Alexander shares in this book will ignite a vision and passion for you. I hope the vision you receive will be a beginning for your school and community to follow the plan he has cast that will make a positive difference in the lives and success of the children you educate in the years to come. Bob's ideas are solid, his approach is right, his statistics are proven, so the results are predetermined. *The Teacher Trap* will help you make a positive difference in the lives of children who one day can make a positive difference in America and the world.

Zig Ziglar
Author/Motivational Teacher

acknowledgements

As a high school football, baseball and basketball coach, I know first hand that games are won
or lost as a team. It is the responsibility of the
coach to blend the unique talents and abilities of
each individual into one heartbeat—a team. The
same is true with writing a book. This book is the
combined effort of uniquely talented and gifted
individuals working together so that the desired
results would be achieved. I am happy to report
the mission has been accomplished, and I am
grateful for their contributions.

First of all, to my parents James and Juanita
Alexander, who taught me the true meaning of
love, honor and respect.

To my wife Pattie, who is my ray of joy, hope
and inspiration.

To our children Britton, Brad, Ashley and
Stephanie. This book was written so you would

have a better opportunity to lead a happy, prosperous and fulfilling life.

Many thanks to the hundreds of teachers, administrators and parents who returned the surveys that were given out in your community. Your feedback provided the foundation for this book.

A heartfelt thanks goes to David Walton for sharing his educational experiences of thirty-nine years. Your contributions have validated the need we have in America to teach the principles we discuss in this book.

To my friend and mentor Jim Norman. Your ability to gather information, analyze the problem and offer workable solutions continues to amaze me. Thanks for all of your encouragement.

A very special thanks goes to Julie Norman for taking a mountain of material and condensing it into a powerful manuscript. Your skills are unparalleled.

My gratitude also goes to Laurie Magers for proofreading the book and providing honest feedback on ways to improve. Your suggestions are always appreciated and most helpful.

I also want to thank my long time friend Teresa Lowe for editing the final manuscript. Your expertise has greatly contributed to this work.

Many thanks to Mary-Frances Burt for designing the cover and formatting the book. Your creative ideas, suggestions and advice have been invaluable.

To my friend and mentor Zig Ziglar for entrusting me with the manufacturing and distribution rights to his I CAN Character Curriculum. It continues to be the best program in America to positively impact our children.

To all the great teachers who taught me, the ones I taught with, and the ones who continue to teach today, may you continue to bless others as you have blessed me. You are my heroes.

And finally, a big thanks to all of you for purchasing this book. I hope it provides you with a clear and concise roadmap for building character in our most precious commodity—our kids.

And now, let's begin to break free from the trap!

Bob Alexander

The perception is that the current state of education in America is horrendous. There are so many causes and contributing factors to the mess that it's almost impossible to list them all. Since 1988, I have been travelling all over this country working with teachers, administrators, and the private sector, and I have seen some incredibly bad situations. I have also seen some incredible success stories.

I began my professional career as an educator. I've been a teacher, a coach, and a high school administrator. I'm also a parent trying to raise four children, ages 13 to 21, in the most challenging educational environment in the history of our nation. I know first hand about the pressures and problems that face today's children and the educators who attempt to teach them. I know about them because I have lived them. I know what it feels like as a teacher to counsel a child who does not understand why his father abuses his mother. As a coach, I have experienced seeing a child's heartbreak in my office because his mother had a different man in the house three times a week. As an administrator, I know the fear of receiving a bomb threat at school, and having to place 1200 students in the parking lot during the blistering hot weather in August. I can still feel the frustration of having to wait more than an hour for a parent to come get his child after an out-of-town basketball game, and, when he got there, the parent was drunk or high on drugs. I can vividly recall the time that I had to physically take a knife away from a boy who was about to use it on a girl. I can still feel the horror I experienced in taking a gun away from a boy who threatened to kill a teacher friend of mine the next period. Although it has been several years ago, I still am reminded of the time I gave CPR to a 65-year-old traveling salesman who dropped to the floor outside my office at school and later died of a massive stroke. Yes, I have been there and done that. *The Teacher Trap* is a book about the things I've learned from my experience, and it offers a practical solution for the real goal of education: Preparing young people for life!

Part of this book will focus on the problems that face American educators, just to demonstrate how difficult these problems are. There are five major players in the educational puzzle: The Student, The Parent, The Teacher, The Administrator, and The Government. Take a close look at this list and tell me who is in the middle? It appears to be the teacher. Now you know why I call this book *The Teacher Trap*. The teacher is trapped in the middle of conflicting perceptions and motivations. Students, parents, administrators, and government agencies all have perceptions about what the problems of education are. Unfortunately, each group has different solutions for those problems and many of the solutions can't be reconciled. Here are 12 of the most popular perceived solutions:

1) Vouchers
2) Hire better teachers
3) Hire more teachers
4) Fire incompetent teachers
5) Hire better administrators
6) Hire more administrators
7) Fire incompetent administrators
8) More government involvement
9) Less government involvement
10) Get parents more involved
11) Get troublesome parents out of the way
12) Put more discipline in the classroom

The first part of *The Teacher Trap* will explore the problems, perceptions, and proposed solutions in some detail. I do it only to demonstrate how complicated it will be to solve all the problems of modern education. The sad part is that while adults try to find political, social, and economic solutions for the problems of education, there are millions of children being brought along with sub-standard skills who will be unprepared to compete in a high-tech world. The real point of *The Teacher Trap* is that children must be educated and some kind of solution must be found NOW! The teacher is trapped in the middle of many opposing forces yet must still do the job. The teacher is trapped in the middle but is still the soldier on the frontline of education. Regardless of what politicians and parents do to improve the situation, teachers have to work with what they have today.

The Teacher Trap is written for teachers who know they have a difficult challenge and still accept the responsibility of being great teachers. There are thousands of teachers who still believe in the educational process and are committed to providing a quality education. These teachers are the real American heroes, and because I had a few of these, I am able to read, write and do math. *The Teacher Trap* provides a simple solution for teachers to be difference-makers in the lives of their students.

We've all heard the analogy about why it's more important to teach people to fish than to give them a fish. If you give them a fish, you feed them for a day. If you teach them how to fish, you feed them for a lifetime. The solution I am presenting in *The Teacher Trap* is designed to help kids learn how to fish for a lifetime. I know from experience that kids who are motivated and have been taught some basic principles of character are able to rise above their circumstances and be successful. *The Teacher Trap* will present absolute proof of this truth by providing the statistical facts and actual case histories that back it up.

The Teacher Trap will provide a simple alternative plan that teachers can use in spite of being trapped in what appears to be a no-win situation. There is a way a dedicated teacher can rise above the fray and accomplish the most important objective: Preparing the child for life. *The Teacher Trap* provides an alternative method for accomplishing this goal.

chapter one

The Kids

In the *Alice in Wonderland* classic by Lewis Carroll, a rabbit scurries about carrying a large clock constantly lamenting that he is late, very late, for a very important date. The rabbit can't seem to remember what he is late for or why he's going wherever he's going. The only certain thing is that he is concerned about it. As a matter of fact, he is very worried about it and is in a state of high anxiety! The rabbit is so worried he's sweating and trembling. He REALLY wants to get where he needs to go. He just can't seem to remember where that might be. The rabbit's dilemma is similar to the education dilemma in America. A whole lot of people are running around the country wringing their hands in concern about the educational system. But few of them seem to remember the direction they need to go, and worse—how they will get there. There is no common vision. Solomon, the wisest man who ever lived, said that the people would perish because of a lack of vision. How important is a vision? A little church in England sums it up with a plaque on the wall that says, "A vision without a task is but a dream. A task without a dream is but drudgery. But a vision with a task is the hope of the world." How important is hope? How important is hope for our children? I think you will agree it is vitally important.

In addition to the children in school, there are four groups directly involved in the education process: Parents, Teachers, School Administrators, and Politicians. One thing can be said about each group: They are all very concerned about the state of our educational system and, like the rabbit, they REALLY want to get where they need to go. There just isn't much agreement about where things need to go or how to get there. There is no common vision.

Everyone has his own opinion about why and how our educational systems are failing for many school children. The list of culprits and reasons is long and includes:

Irresponsible parents
Irresponsible children
Irresponsible teachers
Irresponsible school administrators
Irresponsible politicians
Inadequate funding
Inadequate facilities
Inadequate curriculum
Standardized testing
Inadequate testing
Teen promiscuity
Drugs
Alcohol
Gang violence
Poor discipline
Holes in the ozone layer

Actually, I've never heard anyone blame educational problems on holes in the ozone layer, so I thought I would be the first to do it. I'm sure someone would have already done so if they had thought of it. The point is that there are plenty of things to blame problems on and very few things to praise. Unfortunately, there is at least some truth in everything on that list and the solutions for each problem seem to be beyond the ability of any one person or group to find. The crisis, however, can't wait for all these problems to be eliminated or corrected. The crisis is that children must be educated now and prepared to take their places in a competitive world. The future of our nation and the world depends on it.

The teacher and the student are on the front line of this educational war and are trapped in the middle between the other groups, Parents, Administrators and Politicians. You may wonder why I have included parents with the administrators and the politicians. You would think that parents should be on the front line of the battle with the children and the teachers. Sadly, this is not always the case. While there are many parents who take an active role in their children's education, there are far too many who don't. Schools for many American parents are merely extensions of the day-care system and a place their kids go during the day. Only when their kids are in crisis do these parents surface and become involved. By then their child is usually in big trouble and really struggling.

I believe the children and the teachers are caught in the middle, and if the children are to be educated in spite of all the problems and distractions, the teachers will have to find a way to make it happen. Many teachers have surrendered, just as many children have surrendered. The frustration of teachers has been building for decades as they have lost their classrooms to a host of educational infections. Some of our finest teachers have left the profession and there is no disagreement from me that they are missed in our schools by the children who need them. However, there are still many thousands of excellent teachers who believe in their calling and their profession and want to make a difference in the lives of their students. They live and work in The Teacher Trap and do the best they can with what they have.

For the past decade I have worked with hundreds of school systems and thousands of teachers. I know them well and I have heard their problems. I have listened to their solutions and I have walked in their shoes. I've written *The Teacher Trap* to illuminate the problems of education and to offer a solution that teachers and children can implement together to improve the educational processes. I've become convinced that the total solution will be a long time coming because of educational politics and conflicting agendas of special interests that have little to do with education. Something has to happen to begin to change the way things are being done and it has to happen in the classroom. It's up to the teachers and the students to begin to climb out of this trap on their own. It is the only immediate solution I can see that is practical and possible. If the teachers and students can figure it out, maybe the politicians can too.

In my work with teachers over the years I have surveyed them for their opinions on the state of education. They have eagerly shared their views with me. I've generally asked them the same questions:

1) What do you consider the biggest roadblocks in education?

2) What one thing could parents do to help you be a better teacher?

3) What are the three most important qualities students need to be successful?

4) In spite of your challenges, why do you choose to teach?

These may not be the most sophisticated questions in the world but they get to the heart of things pretty fast. *The Teacher Trap* will discuss the questions and the answers to each as the book moves forward. Right now I want to focus on question #4: In spite of your challenges, why do you choose to teach? Please listen to some of the responses I've received and I know you will understand why there is still hope for American education. Here is a sample of what some real teachers are saying, in spite of their frustration and low pay:

"I want to make a positive difference in the youth of America! I love learning and helping others..."

"I love the innocent laugh of a child."

"I know I can make a difference in someone's life. I often say my being a good teacher is based on how dedicated I am to doing whatever it takes to unlock a child's mind to learning."

"I love children and I want to contribute to their future!"

"I love it when the 'light bulb' goes on and I know learning has taken place."

"I believe I can make a difference—maybe not in all children, but in at least one..."

"Because there is no feeling like that of seeing kids accomplish a difficult task for the first time."

"Because it's what I do best!"

Would you agree these are some powerful comments? I find them to be very typical of what MOST teachers feel and believe. Now, I'm sure there are plenty of bad teachers out there who probably shouldn't be teaching, but I haven't met many of them. As a matter of fact, the teachers I've worked with want to make something happen and I believe there are enough of them teaching to begin to turn things around. All they need is a little bit of help and a little bit of freedom. If they can get it, they can survive The Teacher Trap.

Just because a teacher wants to make a difference doesn't mean he can do it without a bit of help and some good tools. The pressures and educational roadblocks frequently seem too high to hurdle. Teachers have shared their concerns with me and have let me know what they think the real problems are. Let's quickly summarize some of the major things they mention:

Lack of parental support: This is probably the number one concern of teachers today. The list of problems related to this issue is almost endless. I will deal with this in more detail in a subsequent chapter because it is a huge challenge.

Lack of persistence and courage: Today's children have things too easy and want to have everything spoon-fed to them. Too many children are spoiled and see any stumbling block as a mountain impossible to climb. Unfortunately, technology, as great as it is, has contributed to this problem by making our kids lazy.

Low morality: It's not something society wants to admit but many teachers believe the moral values of American society have crumbled and are decimating young people in unprecedented numbers.

Overcrowded classrooms: Some teachers are being forced to teach more children in a room than is practical and kids are lost in the process.

Inadequate structure at home: Children are doing what they want to do at home and staying up too late. They come to school tired and exhausted from staying up watching television or playing computer games. A mind must be rested and fresh to learn.

Excessive emphasis on test scores: A farmer will tell you that you don't fatten a hog by weighing it. You also don't make a child smarter by testing him over and over again. Many school systems seem to believe higher test scores are more important than real education of students. Obviously, this is a very complex issue and there must be a middle ground that would work better.

Politics: There is a lack of support from the outside. Those who are far removed forget the child as they wage political campaigns.

Negative teacher attitudes: Even good teachers are susceptible to forming negative attitudes because of their many frustrations. This can't be tolerated.

Packed curriculum: Teachers feel their curriculum is too busy and attempts to teach too much non-essential information. This detracts from the subjects students really need to learn to become successful adults.

These are most of the real problems teachers have as they attempt to educate their students. Obviously, the problems are many and the problems are complicated. Does this mean things can't change? Does this mean teachers are doomed to failure? Absolutely not! There is a way out of The Teacher Trap and it is a way that is practical and possible. Three things must be taught:

Honesty
Accepting Responsibility
Respect for Self and Others

These are time-honored qualities of successful people and they are three things our children need to understand and PRACTICE on a daily basis. If a child is grounded in these three qualities, he can lift himself up in life and become educated. The good news is that these qualities can be learned and developed. All the student needs to learn these qualities is the help of a good teacher who wants to make a difference. *The Teacher Trap* will explain how to make it happen.

chapter two

The Parents

The parents of American school children are frustrated with the educational problems in the public schools and want some significant improvements. Education has become a major issue in American politics and it is fueled by parents' concerns that their children are not being properly educated. There is a sense that the tax dollars being collected should be enough to produce quality education but the evidence is not seen, thus a rise in private schools and home schooling. There are many concerned parents who take an active role in the education of their children. Unfortunately, there are far more who don't. As a matter of fact, the number one problem of most teachers is the parents of the children they are trying to teach.

South Brunswick, New Jersey—*Police said a tied soccer game between 8 and 9 year old girls ended in a brawl among their parents Sunday after a disagreement over where a coach was standing...the argument escalated into a fistfight with as many as a dozen parents and coaches involved. No children were involved. Even after police arrived, parents were still yelling at each other...*

—The Associated Press,
September 10, 2000

The fight was just one case of parental rage at youth sporting events that year. On Jan 25, 2002, a hockey dad was indicted on manslaughter charges in the beating death of another father at a game in Massachusetts.

News articles like these are too familiar. Although this example came from youth sports, these behaviors overlap into our schools. Society as a whole is taking a hard look at the schools and teachers who educate American children, and many of the parents are behaving like children themselves. In this news report of the feuding parents, the children actually behaved like adults because they didn't take part in the fight.

I wish stories of parents acting like fools were rare, but they aren't. Any teacher in America can tell you story after story about problems with parents and the negative effect these problems have on the children. To drive home this point, let me share with you some actual teacher comments about the parents they deal with. Teachers provided the following responses to the question: "What do you consider the biggest roadblock in educating students?"

"Discipline in school is difficult and the parents are exhibiting the same behavior as the 'problem' child in the classroom."

"Parents' negative talk and lack of positive involvement with their child and the school. (They don't care enough about themselves, each other, their family, or anyone.)"

"Lack of parental support. It's essential for parents to encourage their children to attend school daily and to be respectful."

"Parents! Because they won't take responsibility for their shortcomings. Also, they allow the schools to take the 'societal beating' they should be getting."

"Lack of support from parents. Parents expect teachers to 'do it all.'"

"Lack of parental support in terms of discipline, respecting authority, and completing class work and homework."

"Parental apathy."

"Lack of parental support. In most cases my students are so lacking in values and responsibility because they do not see them demonstrated at home. It's a sad message when you schedule a parent and student for a conference and the parent is a 'no show.'"

"Students are not prepared mentally because they don't get enough sleep. Parents don't care if they do their homework. Children are allowed to watch TV, play video games far too late—too much, too long."

Sadly, I could fill up this book with quotes like these. I believe the thing fundamentally wrong with the American education system is that children are not being taught the old-fashioned values and principles that everyone took for granted in the not so distant past.

What happened to pledging allegiance to the flag, a moment of silence, standing at attention when the national anthem is played? The next time you go to a ballgame and the anthem is played, watch and see how many parents do not take their caps off. See how few place their hands over their hearts. You will be amazed. There are many reasons for this disaster, but the bottom line is that there has been a steady decline in moral values and respect for others for the past 30 to 40 years. We have now produced a couple of generations that have failed to learn all of the lessons they need about honesty and accepting responsibility.

Cooking a Frog

There is an old story about cooking a frog. The idea is that if you put a live frog in a pot of cold water and put it on a burner, the frog will be slowly cooked and will never attempt to jump out of the pot. The gradual heating of the water will be slow and the frog won't notice the change until it's too late. That is the nature of negative change and it is specifically the case with the parents of today. Let's take a look at how this frog got cooked.

Human values are embraced by society when society as a whole accepts those values as being the truth. Whatever the society believes regarding values determines how they will behave and act. For example, if society as a whole believes it is shameful to divorce a spouse, then there won't be many divorces. Couples with problems will try harder to solve them before they throw away their marriages. Another example might be that if society as a whole believes that abortion is more than a choice but is actually the taking of a human life, there will be fewer abortions—even if abortions continue to be legal. Society does what it believes.

You don't have to look back very far to find a generation that had a set of values in stark contrast to 21st century values. Coincidentally, in the past year or two, the generation I'm referring to has been widely celebrated and saluted. I'm talking about "The Greatest Generation," as NBC news anchor Tom Brokaw described them in his best selling book of the same title: The generation that fought and won WWII. This generation was the most pivotal of all the 20th century generations. They represented the best of the best, but ironically they were also the generation that marked the beginning of the move away from the traditional, biblical values that formed the basis for American culture. In this generation you can find the seeds of greatness as well as the formula for moral decay, and in both cases, these opposites have been passed along to us, their children.

The young men and women who lived, fought, and died in WWII were children of the Depression. They were dirt-poor people who struggled all their lives to earn enough money to survive. They knew hard work and they knew the meaning of perseverance. They also believed three important things about personal values and character:

1) They believed honesty was the basis of strong human relationships.

2) They believed that individuals were responsible for their own actions.

3) They believed that respect was something that had to be earned.

I'm going to be talking about these three core values throughout this book because these are the three values that have dramatically eroded over the past 50 years. I bring them up here because there is no question that the WWII generation had a strong grip on these values as it is demonstrated by what they accomplished. The problem is this: Somewhere between the WWII generation and the society of the year 2002, these three values have been diluted, ignored, overlooked or completely denied by varying segments of American society. It happened to us very slowly. It was like cooking a frog.

The WWII generation possessed these three values to a high degree but every generation since has moved gradually away from them. This is a horrifying truth, and unfortunately, the cause of the erosion of these values also may be placed at the feet of the "greatest generation." The irony of this is overwhelming. How could the best of America also provide the seeds of disaster? Simple. They didn't want their children to live a life as hard as theirs and they began to prop them up and protect them from some of life's hard lessons. They wanted their children to have advantages they never had. They succeeded.

The children of the WWII generation are the people identified as "Baby Boomers." These people became the first spoiled group of children after WWII and they rewarded their parents' hard work and dedication by creating the drug culture and the protests of the 1960's. Many Baby Boomers became revolutionaries in a sense and the three qualities that so characterized their parents were not as evident in their lives. Many children of the WWII generation were less honest, less responsible, and didn't respect anything! They were partakers of the "if it feels good do it" approach to life.

Before I go any further with this discussion, I need to make some qualifying remarks. It's not my intent to condemn any generation of Americans with an across the board indictment. But I am trying to show how we got this frog cooked over the past 50 years and there is no doubt that traditional values began to shrink with the advent of the Baby Boomers. The Baby Boomers were the first generation after WWII to publicly use drugs and participate in openly promiscuous relationships, and it was with this generation that divorce statistics began to explode. Baby Boomers were not a happy generation of people. They took themselves very seriously as they protested and waged political war against authority of every form. They found hypocrisy in every American institution and many of them "dropped out" and indulged themselves in their selfishness. These children of the "Greatest Generation" launched the first broad attack against traditional values and prevailed in many ways.

Now that I've criticized the Baby Boomers so severely, I need to also lift them up. Once they recovered from their rebelliousness of the 1960's, they became a highly productive generation. The Baby Boomers largely built the economy we enjoy today, but the traditional values they began to abandon have never recovered. This generation that fought for civil rights and justice for the disadvantaged also introduced the idea that people may not be responsible for their own actions and may be "victims."

The Baby Boomers had children and their children have had children. Along the way, America has changed dramatically. We have become the most technologically advanced nation on earth, enjoying the most productive economic engine in the history of the world. Even with the fall of our economy in 2001, people are making more money than ever before and our standard of living is the envy of the planet. Yet, we have also become other things that are not so admirable.

We have become a nation of questionable moral character. Divorce rates are higher than ever and drug use among high school students has hit epidemic proportions. The three characteristics so important to personal integrity (honesty, accepting responsibility, and respecting the rights of others) have been steadily eroding for the past 40 years. Today, the absence of these qualities in young people is frightening. We have created a culture in which nobody is responsible for anything and our children are learning the lessons well. The problem is not the killer, it's the gun's fault. The problem is not that people choose to smoke, it's the fault of the people who make the cigarettes. We are a society of victims.

What's the Point?

What teachers are seeing in American class-rooms is a generation of children that believe honesty and truth are opinions. They believe if anything unpleasant happens to them, it is somebody else's fault. They also show little respect for the rights or property of others, but tenaciously cling to their own. Like society, these children are a bundle of contradictions whose primary objective is to do what they want to do, when they want to do it. The teachers, who have the challenge of educating these youngsters, have the most difficult jobs in the world, and their challenge is made much harder because of the parents of these students.

Teachers see the attitudes of parents reflected in their students and they know that when a child needs discipline, they will be lucky to be supported by the parents of the child. Many years ago a teacher could easily get control of a discipline problem by threatening to call and report the child to his parents. Today, the children have reversed this strategy. If the teacher does something they don't like, they will report the teacher to their parents. The lack of parental support is one of the major problems for teachers to overcome and every teacher lives in fear of irrational parents coming to school to protest their teaching methods.

No group of people knows more about the condition of the average American family than the teachers of America. Most teachers know their students well, and in knowing the students, they know the parents. When children come to school tired, irritable and totally unmotivated to learn, it is obvious to teachers the children are not being supervised at home. Far too many parents are apathetic about their children's education and sincerely believe education should be the sole responsibility of the school system. It is not unusual for some parents to be baffled as to why the school is reporting a problem to them about their children.

By far, however, the biggest problem teachers see with parents is their inability to be positive role models for their children. Far too many children do not see the basic qualities of honesty and accepting responsibility in their own parents. They see parents calling in sick to work when they aren't really sick. They see parents telling lies and they see parents making excuses for their own behavior. It is no mystery to teachers why it is so difficult to educate children today. The children have not received the proper training at home. When the kids come to school, they are surrounded by other children who are lacking the same training. The obvious conclusion for them to draw is that they and their peers have the correct outlook on life.

I've been pretty tough on parents in this chapter and I need to acknowledge that there are still many good parents who take an active interest in the education of their children. They demand the best from their kids and they support the hard work of the teachers charged with educating their children. But these excellent parents fight the same problems the teachers face. Too many parents do not set the proper examples their children need and they are sending children out into the world lacking the basic values they need to achieve. Human beings copy other human beings and children are highly influenced by their peers. When high percentages of the peer group believe and agree that honesty is just an opinion, even the best trained children can become confused.

There are countless examples of good parents having serious problems with their children because the cumulative sickness of their children's peers finally overpowered the positive lessons they learned at home from their parents. The solution for many of these parents has been to enroll their children in private schools that actively teach and expect moral values to be demonstrated by the students and that also demand parental involvement with the education process. Some private schools demand this involvement so strongly they will refuse admission to students of parents who do not agree to participate.

There are other reasons that the education system in America is severely challenged and we will discuss them in subsequent chapters. The other problems are important and they are real, but none of them approaches the importance of the parental problem. The responsibility for the basic values of children begins and ends with parents. Institutions and schools should only be charged with affirming the values children should have learned at home from their parents. Sadly, that is not the case. The world has turned upside down in many ways since the "Greatest Generation" saved the world from Nazi oppression. Somehow the frog got cooked and the result is sitting in the classrooms of America in the form of students in desperate need of some basic values to firmly anchor their lives. The teacher is bearing the brunt of this huge problem and not getting much help to solve it.

That is sad for our children and for our nation. Things must change.

chapter three

The Teachers

Betty decided she wanted to become a teacher when she was in the tenth grade. She had experienced a life changing influence in the form of her 10th grade history teacher, Mrs. Joan Peterson. Joan Peterson was in her early 50's when Betty came to her class and had been teaching history for 25 years. Joan, too, had always wanted to be a teacher because she wanted to impact the minds and hearts of young people who might go forth from her class and change the world.

Before Betty was placed in Joan Peterson's history class, school was just a place to go and something she had to do. You couldn't say that Betty was excited about her own education. Betty was smart and made above average grades, but did so with little serious effort. Then, Joan Peterson entered her life and everything changed. Attending Mrs. Peterson's class became the highlight of her day—every day. Because of Joan Peterson's influence, Betty completely reshaped her view of education. She began to see her classes as tools that would help her succeed in life, rather than as a series of boring lectures. Joan Peterson made history live for Betty and Betty decided there could be no higher calling than to become a teacher herself. Betty wanted to impact the lives of young people in the same way Joan Peterson had impacted hers!

After graduating from high school, Betty went to college, seeking a degree in Education. Her family was not financially able to carry all of Betty's college expenses, so it was necessary for her to work part-time to support herself and help pay for her tuition and books. Having to work also restricted the number of classes she could take each semester, so it took Betty six years to graduate and earn her teaching certification. It was a difficult six years and required a lot of sacrifice, effort and determination. Mostly, it was Betty's memory of Joan Peterson that gave her the courage and the persistence to stay the course and reach her goal. Betty's graduation and the attainment of her teaching certificate was the most joyful and satisfying event in her life. She was finally ready to begin her teaching career and become another Joan Peterson. She was ready to change the lives of her students and prepare them for success!

It didn't take Betty long to find her first teaching position, although it was not with the school district she had hoped for. She was hired to teach the fourth grade in a suburban elementary school located in a middle-class neighborhood. She was excited and she made plans to attend an orientation session for new teachers in the district.

At her orientation Betty met many other new teachers coming into the district for the first time. Some were experienced teachers coming from other schools and some were new to the profession, as she was. She enjoyed the orientation, but left it a bit fearful and confused. Much of the orientation involved warnings about legal threats and liability that could be placed on teachers for improper behavior. She also heard a lot of gossip among some of the more experienced teachers about horror stories and things she could expect when she finally got into her classroom. Most of the complaints and gossip centered on two topics: parental apathy and the politics of school administrators.

On her first day in the classroom, Betty was anxious to get started. In college she had done her required practice teaching, but this would be "her" class. She could teach in her own style and not worry about having to please someone else for the sake of earning a good evaluation. Betty had a lot of good ideas and was very creative in her preparation. For the first few days and weeks everything was going well until she felt the need to discipline one of her students who was habitually late to class and rarely did homework assignments. Betty sent a note of concern home to the child's parents, informing them that their child would be detained after class to do extra work until improvements were made.

The first thing that happened was a formal complaint filed by the parents alleging that the action being taken against their child was unreasonable and unfair. The parents complained that their child did not "like" Betty and had been complaining about being "picked on" because Betty didn't like the child. Betty was shocked and dismayed when her principal called her in to discuss the complaint and inform her that a meeting had been scheduled for the parents to come in and discuss the matter with her. The principal said she would also attend the meeting.

The meeting was a disaster for Betty. She was appalled by the things the parents said about her. Nothing they said was factual or specific. Nothing they said could be proved or disproved. Nothing they said had any basis in the truth and she was highly offended by the parents' attitudes and the entire proceeding. After an hour of tense discussion, the principal thanked the parents for coming in and assured them that their complaints would be taken seriously and the "situation" would be monitored to insure their child received the best education possible. The parents nodded, frowned one last time at Betty and left. Betty looked to her principal for sympathy and support, but all she saw was a blank, emotionless expression on her face.

Betty's principal advised her that she was going to have to put a review letter in her records, but it would be removed after one year if there were no future incidents or complaints of a similar nature. The principal did acknowledge that the parents were probably being unreasonable but they had to take complaints seriously because they feared legal action. Betty was crushed and humiliated.

The child in question became a bigger problem as time went by. Homework assignments were poorly done and the child developed a negative, insolent attitude. Betty was forced to document everything the child did to protect herself against any new complaints the child's parents might make against her. Teachers that Betty worked with gave her lots of advice about how to cover herself and guard against future attacks on her job. Betty's first year of teaching was nothing like she thought it would be. Her dream of becoming another Joan Peterson somehow got swallowed up in fear and self-protection. She spent countless nights worrying about her career, her students, and whether or not she had chosen the right profession. And she got to experience all of this misery for an annual salary of $23,500!

Betty taught school for another two years and quit. She became fed up with low pay, politics, and parents who seemed to be more interested in attacking her than improving the education of their own children. Betty decided that the world of Joan Peterson no longer existed and she was unwilling to stay in a system that seemed so short-sighted.

•

Betty is not a real person and neither was Joan Peterson. I created this story based on thousands of Bettys who became teachers and found themselves mired in an educational nightmare that crushed their dreams. In real life, some of the

Bettys quit, but some of them keep on teaching in spite of the difficulty and the frustration they face every day in their classrooms. Here is a recent news article that will paint the picture very clearly:

•

Study finds lying, cheating among high-school students

By GISELE DURHAM, Associated Press
LOS ANGELES (October 16, 2000 9:28 a.m. EDT)

Many of the nation's high school students lie and cheat and some have shown up for class drunk, according to preliminary results of a nationwide teen character study released Monday.

Seven in 10 students surveyed admitted cheating on a test at least once in the past year, and nearly half said they had done so more than once, according to the nonprofit, nonpartisan Joseph & Edna Josephson Institute of Ethics.

"This data reveals a hole in the moral ozone," said Michael Josephson, founder and president of the Marina Del Rey-based organization.

On the other hand, the results were not significantly worse than on the last test in 1998—the first time that has happened since the group began testing in 1992.

"The good news appears that it's peaked," Josephson said. "The bad news is that it's horribly high."

The "Report Card on the Ethics of American Youth" found that 92 percent of the 8,600 students surveyed lied to their parents in the past year. Seventy-eight percent said they had lied to a teacher, and more than one in four said they would lie to get a job.

Nearly one in six students said they had shown up for class drunk at least once in the past year. Sixty-eight percent admitted they hit someone because they were angry. Nearly half—47 percent—said they could get a gun if they wanted to.

Josephson said the results amounted to the formula for a "toxic cocktail" involving "kids who think it's OK to hit someone when they're angry, who may be drunk at school when they do it, and who can also get their hands on a gun."

Josephson stopped short of assigning blame to a particular group, but he said parents, teachers and coaches need to pay special attention because they have the most significant interactions with youngsters.

"I'm not saying there aren't some out there doing their best," he said. "But if all three were doing their best, we wouldn't have this problem."

The survey, conducted this year, involved students in grades nine through 12 in public and private schools. Participating schools handed out surveys with 57 questions that students could submit anonymously.

The results had a margin of error of plus or minus 3 percentage points. The high school results, along with those for middle schools, will be included in a series of three final reports to be released later this year.

•

When I read reports like the one I just quoted, it sends chills up and down my spine. The findings of this report are right on target, in my opinion. I travel to schools all across America every year and I visit personally with teachers in every kind of teaching environment. I assure you, the attitudes reflected in the Josephson Institute of Ethics report is an accurate reflection of what I hear. These are serious problems of culture and involve basic principles of morality. Kids are not learning these deceptive attitudes and practices from their teachers. They are bringing them to school with them!

I don't think I have to spend a lot of time trying to convince you or prove to you that the American public education system is perceived as a wreck. I think most people recognize there is some truth and proof of that. Our children are not being satisfactorily educated. What disturbs me is that teachers frequently get an unfair share of the criticism for this disaster. On February 22, 2000, U. S. Secretary of Education Richard W. Riley delivered a speech to an audience at Southern High School, Durham North Carolina. Here is an excerpt from that speech about what Secretary Riley had to say about improving teacher quality:

•

Improving Teacher Quality

Improving teacher quality is at the heart of our national effort to achieve excellence in the classroom. This comes at a time when the very structure of education is going through a profound change. With knowledge all around us, available anytime and anywhere, the role of the teacher is going to be fundamentally transformed in the 21st Century.

In the future, schools will be more fluid, teachers more adaptable and flexible, and students will be more accountable as the task of learning becomes *theirs. **The challenge of the modern classroom is its increasing diversity and the skills that this diversity requires of teachers.** This is why we need to do some new thinking when it comes to the teaching profession.*

We need a dramatic overhaul of how we recruit, prepare, induct and retain good teachers. The status quo is not good enough. And we must revamp professional development as we know it. New distance learning models can be a powerful new tool to give teachers more opportunities to be better teachers.

Our efforts to improve education will rise or fall on the quality of our teaching force, and higher education has the defining role in preparing the next generation of teachers. I ask leaders in higher education across the nation to please make this their mission.

•

I'm concerned that the former highest education official in the U. S. Government believed: **"The challenge of the modern classroom is its increasing diversity and the skills that this diversity requires of teachers."** In my opinion, this is an unbelievable state of denial to the real problems that exist. And if there is one thing I know, it's this: If you can't diagnose the real disease, you can't cure it. The disease, Mr. Secretary, is "character cancer," as evidenced by the Josephson ethics study. Let's look at those study highlights one more time:

• **_Cheating._** 71% of all high school students admit they cheated on an exam at least once in the past 12 months (45% said they did so two or more times).

• **_Lying._** 92% lied to their parents in the past 12 months (79% said they did so two or more times); 78% lied to a teacher (58% two or more times); more than one in four (27%) said they would lie to get a job.

• **_Stealing._** 40% of males and 30% of females say they stole something from a store in the past 12 months.

• **_Drunk at School._** Nearly one in six (16%) say they have been drunk in school during the past year (9% said they were drunk two or more times).

• **_Propensity Toward Violence._** 68% say they hit someone because they were angry in the past year (46% did so at least twice), and nearly half (47%)

said they could get a gun if they wanted to (for males: 60% say they could get a gun).

If these problems are the result of classroom diversity, someone needs to explain the connection to me. I don't get it.

There is one issue that just about everyone in the education field agrees with. There is a coming teacher shortage that will present a tremendous problem for our schools unless something is done. I do agree with Secretary Riley's comment that, "We need a dramatic overhaul of how we recruit, prepare, induct and retain good teachers." Solving the problem of the teacher shortage must be done in two ways:

1) More people have to want to be teachers;

2) The people who already teach must continue to teach.

Unfortunately, the negative experiences of teachers in public schools, coupled with low pay scales, impact both ends of the solution!

The Teacher Shortage

Listen to the comments of Sandra Feldman, President of the American Federation of Teachers, in an article she published in October 2000:

"How can we attract more young people to teaching? Become a teacher? Not likely. That's how most New York City teenagers responded to a recent poll asking them if they would be interested in a career as a city teacher. Although the majority of the young people, who included high school and college students, felt positive about the services their own teachers had provided, only 24 percent found teaching in New York City schools very, or even fairly, appealing.

"There is little doubt that these results would be repeated in cities across the country—and who can blame the kids? Why should they want to enter a field where their work will get little recognition and their salaries will never approach what other professionals make?

"So it's not hard to understand why young people—and talented ones in particular— don't even consider teaching. But the growing teacher shortage gives a new urgency to the situation, especially since it comes at a time when we are working hard to raise student achievement—and beginning to succeed.

Will we be able to attract high-quality young teachers to public schools—and especially to schools in urban areas?"

I don't know about you but this is not good news in view of the fact that it's estimated we will need 2,000,000 new teachers to staff our bulging school systems. Here's what Ms. Feldman said about this in 1998:

"Salaries, as any teacher will tell you, are not the main problem. A spotlight has been turned on teachers this school year, illuminating some dark corners of the world in which they work—inadequate pay, little professional support, difficult working conditions. It's also caused a sudden flurry of concern: Over the next ten years, we will need to hire 2.2 million new teachers. Where will we find them?

"Right now, the attrition rate is 22 percent overall in the first three years and nearly 50 percent for teachers in urban schools…And salaries, as any teacher will tell you, are hardly the main problem. There are all the small—and large—things that make the job tough. Not having enough materials and books and supplies, for example. Teachers often spend hundreds of dollars of their own money to make sure their students have what they need.

"We talk a lot about computers, about the sophisticated and powerful technology that links us to the remotest parts of the globe. Yet most teachers, if they want to call a parent about how her kid is doing in math, have to go down the hall and wait in line for a telephone.

"I've been in countless classrooms where I've asked youngsters how many would like to be teachers. Sometimes not a single hand goes up. Do we think bright college students aren't put off by the teacher-bashing they hear and see in the media? Do we think they haven't noticed for themselves the working conditions their teachers had to put up with—and the often lousy pay?

"Young people who want to teach want to help children. They want to do meaningful work, to make a difference. They also want to support families and feel successful."

I believe Ms. Feldman's observations are right on target! I'd like to highlight two of her comments for special attention. She said,

"Do we think bright college students aren't put off by the teacher-bashing they hear and see in the media?"

She also said,

"A spotlight has been turned on teachers this school year, illuminating some dark corners of the world in which they work—inadequate pay, little professional support, difficult working conditions."

I believe there is a public perception of teachers that has been projected and it is not a fair representation of the vast majority of teachers in America. The media, in conjunction with certain political pundits, seem to present unusual, isolated stories and leave the public with the impression that these isolated stories are widespread. There is no question that any profession can produce individuals who shouldn't be doing what they do and teaching is no exception. In fact, there are some teachers who can tell you the exact number of years, months, weeks, days, and minutes they have until they can retire. I mention in my speaking engagements that these so called teachers might as well go ahead and retire now, because they have been semi-retired in their classrooms for years. They could do us all a favor, especially the kids, if they would retire now. And I'm not saying that certain, individual teachers don't need some help. They do. What I am saying, however, is that most of the teachers I know of are hard-working, committed professionals who are trying to do a difficult job in an insane environment.

The National PTA conducted a national survey of parents of public school students and created a demographic analysis of the parents' opinions about problems in public schools. Here is a summary of the survey results:

•

Serious Problems in Schools: A Demographic Analysis

Parents' concerns about their children's schools vary tremendously by demographic group and clear patterns emerge. Parents of children in grades K-5 are consistently more satisfied with their children's schools than are parents of children in grades 6-8 or 9-12, regardless of the income level or education level of the parents. Thus, parents of middle school and high school children are more likely than elementary school parents to report serious problems in their children's schools.

High school parents: For parents of children in grades 9-12, the number one problem cited in their own child's school is "alcohol and drug abuse," reported as a serious problem by 75% of parents. Almost as serious a problem, according to

65% of high school parents, is that "most parents don't know what is going on in the school." In addition, 45% of high school parents report that the "school does not keep parents well-informed."

Middle school parents: For parents of middle school children (grades 6-8), their number one concern is that "most parents don't know what is going on in the school," considered a problem by 59% of these parents. Forty-five percent (45%) cite drug and alcohol abuse, while 33% of these parents feel that the school does not keep parents well-informed.

Elementary school parents: For parents of young children in kindergarten through grade 5, 41% feel that "most parents don't know what is going on in the school." Only 25% of these parents feel that the school does not keep parents well-informed.

•

I'd like to take a thoughtful look at these survey results. Did you notice that the biggest problem in high schools and middle schools relates to drug and alcohol abuse! Coming in right behind drugs and alcohol is the concern that parents don't know what is going on in their children's schools.

Then they say the schools don't do enough to tell parents what is going on! I get the impression that the parents also believe that these issues are the schools' to solve. In response, I ask two questions:

1) What is the parents' role in the drug and alcohol choices their own children are making?

2) Why is it that so many parents don't know what's going on in their children's schools?

You know, I've never worked with a teacher who didn't welcome parental concern and involvement. Most teachers are frustrated by parental apathy to involvement in their child's education. Efforts teachers make to get parents involved are frequently ignored! I also have never met a teacher who was trying to get the students involved in drugs and alcohol. The young people who are taking drugs and drinking alcohol are not doing it because of teaching conditions in their schools. There are other reasons that drive these choices and most of them relate to our overall culture. It's an issue of character.

Where and how young people are developing the character traits that drive their behavior can be hotly debated for a long time. The answer is probably very complicated and diverse. Character is a result of what people believe and human beings start at an early age forming belief principles from their parents. As we get older, the influences that affect our belief principles become more complex, but they begin at home when we are young. By the time a child arrives at school, much of the foundation has been put in place. If a child's moral foundation is weak—and if the child with a weak moral foundation meets others with weak foundations in a school setting—the beliefs they have (or the lack of them) are strengthened and reinforced. There is no doubt the greatest influence on young people, other than their parents, is from their peers. When the entire peer group is deficient in basic character foundations the negative results can become an epidemic. That is what I believe we have in America: A lack of character epidemic.

Teachers have a platform and an opportunity to turn this tide and reverse it. However, to be successful, teachers will need the support of parents, the general public, and the school bureaucrats. Character can be taught and character can be learned because it is a function of what people believe. If people really believe it's wrong to lie, cheat and steal—most of them won't do it. The challenge of teachers today is not just to teach educational basics of reading and math. The nature of character deficiency requires that it be attacked at every point. The schools become a natural, obvious battleground for character education and offer the greatest hope. Most teachers realize the truth of this, but they need the support of parents and school officials to make it happen.

chapter four

Honesty

The heart of this book is that there are three personal qualities that form the foundation of every student's chance to be successful in life: honesty, accepting responsibility, and respect for others. The next three chapters deal with each of these qualities. The problems in our schools are many, but the fundamental need to educate children remains, regardless of political, economic and cultural influences. I believe the vast majority of teachers are up to this challenge and I believe that character education should be the primary weapon in the war. People who are honest, accept responsibility for their own actions, and respect others have the basic tools to be successful in life.

Honesty is the character quality that forms the foundational bedrock of every human being. There is no other issue of character that is more important than honesty, but honesty is not a simple matter. It is not a simple matter because people have the uncanny ability to be untruthful and justify their dishonesty for a variety of reasons, in a variety of ways. Let's examine some of the ways dishonesty manifests itself in the lives of people.

Some instances of honesty and dishonesty are driven by human feelings about the actions of others. Our greatest distortions of truth involve our impulsive reactions to the behavior of other people. Let's face it, each of us has our own view of how we want the events of our lives to play out. We also have no shortage of opinions about how other people should conduct themselves when our lives touch. This may be the most difficult form of honesty to evaluate.

When we don't get what we want, and we believe other people have played a role in our disappointment, it's very easy to distort the truth to ourselves. In psychological terms this form of self-deception is known as *denial.* Don't we all like to develop reasons that our disappointment was not OUR fault? It's more comfortable and easier to blame our disappointment on the actions of others. The first example of blame is in the Biblical account of Adam and Eve in the Garden of Eden. After eating the forbidden fruit, Adam and Eve hid from God. When God found them, He asked why they ate the forbidden morsel. Adam blamed Eve and Eve blamed the snake. A more current example is the now famous story of a person who spilled hot coffee on himself after purchasing it at a McDonald's drive-thru window. He sued McDonald's for making coffee that was too hot!

Another form of honesty involves events and time. It involves what we have done in the past, what we are doing in the present, and what we will do in the future. It is a form of honesty that usually involves events in which we were successful, or events in which we experienced failure of some kind. "Calendar honesty" involves revealing information about personal events that color or influence what others may think of us.

A well-known example of this kind of dishonesty involves some of the statements Vice President Al Gore made during the 2000 presidential campaign. Among other things, Gore claimed to have invented the Internet; he claimed the movie "Love Story" was based on his and his wife Tipper's relationship; he claimed to have been one of the founders of the U. S. Strategic Petroleum Reserve; he claimed he made trips to

Texas to inspect flood disasters with a named government official. It has been well documented that none of these claims were truthful. The motive for Gore's false claims was to create an impression of involvement and experience to build voter confidence in his abilities.

Dishonesty about events usually involves exaggeration that produces deception. When a person relates information about an event from the past, there is usually evidence that the event happened. If there is a distortion of truth, it is usually in the reporting of the details of the event and the person's role in that event. An example might be a middle-aged, overweight gentleman recalling his slimmer, more athletic days playing high school sports. If such a person was prone to exaggeration, his prowess on the playing field might be far more formidable in his mind than the truth would support. In fact, I have known some people that the older they get, the better they were. I imagine you have known people like this, too. Exaggeration, rather than blatant dishonesty, would be the more likely factor in such a case.

However, there are some people who completely fabricate events out of whole cloth. They claim educational credentials they do not have. They claim they have worked for companies that have no record of their employment. They lie about former marriages. They lie about their criminal history. They lie about things they have owned and things they have accomplished. Because such cases are not that rare, the private investigation profession is doing very well. It is the reason employers investigate claims made on employment applications and personal résumés. It is also the reason a well-known football coach was forced to resign after only five days on the job at the University of Notre Dame. He admitted he lied about having a master's degree and about playing years while in college. Even though giving false information happened years ago to make his résumé look good for his first job, it eventually caught up with him. It not only cost him millions of dollars immediately, but more importantly, it damaged his reputation forever.

Human deception is not new. People have been telling lies about themselves and others for as long as history records human behavior. And no person is immune to the tendency to deceive others. It's just that some people do more of it than others and they do it on a much grander scale. What is the difference between people who lie and those who don't? I believe it is a matter of conscience. Some people tell lies and feel guilty about it. Their remorse over their deception produces a genuine regret and they wrestle with conscience and spirit about their duplicity. Others, however, lie with little regret and indeed feel there is no moral imperative to tell the truth. These people almost seem to have a malfunction of conscience and are able to tell lies free from guilt.

The human conscience is a valuable mechanism because it serves as a brake and a safety net against abhorrent behavior. If you are human, you must admit that you have had thoughts that caused you private shame and guilt. Having thoughts that cause us shame and guilt is a natural condition for all people. My personal opinion is that it is a spiritual conflict. Spiritually speaking, it is because of a sin nature we carry as a result of rebellion against God. The human conscience is somehow a link to Godliness and signals guilt to prevent us from moving from thought to action in most instances.

How is it that the consciences of some seem to be impaired or non-existent? There are some people who believe they have never had a conscience because they are unaware of ever experiencing a sense of guilt. I have a good friend who is active in a recovery program for alcoholism and the issue of guilt and remorse is a big part of his recovery. My friend says that when he was young, his conscience performed admirably. Unfortunately, he was able to overcome his guilt frequently enough to do some things that led him down a sad road for many years. It seems that the more he "overruled" his conscience and turned his thoughts into action, the less effective his conscience became. He told me a great analogy that makes it very clear. He said to imagine your conscience being like a sharp rotating shard of metal that is imbedded in your flesh. Whenever you think or do something that is morally or socially wrong, the shard rotates in your flesh causing pain. However, if you repeatedly overrule the pain and succumb to the evil thought or behavior, the shard of metal begins to become smooth and its effect is diminished. Over a long period of time the shard becomes completely smooth and just rotates with no discomfort. At that point the conscience has become ineffective and the poor soul without the brake of conscience is completely subject to his or her own selfishness and wickedness.

I've been discussing conscience because I believe it is a major factor in many of the problems being played out in our culture and in our schools. Conscience is also a product of education, and when our children are taught that they can decide what things are true and what things are not true, I believe conscience is diminished. I am not a psychiatrist, psychologist or mental health professional. I am just a professional educator, a father, and a person who can apply basic common sense to issues that are obvious. Consider the following quote by noted columnist Cal Thomas:

"The failure to teach the presence of absolutes and truth in our schools is what is primarily responsible for the education disaster that nearly everyone now sees or forecasts for the near future.... If a philosophy and worldview once produced generations of young people who could read, write, and think while resisting, for the most part, the temptation to engage in anti-social and personally corrupting behavior, why doesn't it make sense to return to that philosophy and reject the one that has brought us crack cocaine in the school yard and drive-by shootings at the playground?"

I think the point in Thomas' remarks is that there was something we used to teach in our schools and in our society that produced educated, literate, thinking people. The "thing" was honesty and morality. Paul Hein, Jr., M.D., a physician in solo practice and the author of *All Work And No Play,* reflects his fascination with the nature of money and its role in our society.

Listen to the observations Dr. Hein makes about the moral shift that has impacted our children in the past 40 years:

"...In addition to the material aspects of life...there was an obvious moral difference between then and now. Children in school did not, with some regularity, assault one another or their teachers. Metal detectors, even if they existed, would have been unheard of in school. Condoms were not mentioned, much less distributed, in the belief that the innocence of childhood was precious and should be preserved...One could attend a movie without being embarrassed by the language, and listen to a popular song without being incited to kill a policeman."

In the days to which Dr. Hein refers, there was a clear understanding in society about right and wrong. There were absolutes and truths about right and wrong that were taught and they provided a moral rudder for our children and for our society. One of the absolutes and truths taught in American culture was the absolute requirement and expectation to tell the truth! Honesty was expected in personal and private dealings, and anyone who was publicly identified as a liar had a very difficult time. This expectation of honesty from others was so strong it is STILL a quality that people want and demand, but it has diminished in recent years. For many young people, lying is an acceptable act under certain circumstances.

Let's go back to the ethics survey we discussed in Chapter 3. Again, here are the results of the survey taken of students:

• *Cheating.* 71% of all high school students admit they cheated on an exam at least once in the past 12 months (45% said they did so two or more times).

• *Lying.* 92% lied to their parents in the past 12 months (79% said they did so two or more times); 78% lied to a teacher (58% two or more times); more than one in four (27%) said they would lie to get a job.

• *Stealing.* 40% of males and 30% of females say they stole something from a store in the past 12 months.

It is depressing to read these statistics, and even worse to realize the students who gave the answers did so with little or no remorse for their behavior. Such attitudes are not surprising, considering the examples being set by certain leaders and role models of American society. I think most of you can think of many negative role models regarding truthfulness, so I won't waste time detailing their behavior.

Children are not born with full knowledge of exactly what is right and what is wrong. The details and specifics of right and wrong have to be learned. Because the details of right and wrong must be learned, there are diverging opinions as to which details should be taught to our children. Our country is divided between those who believe and support the traditional moral concepts presented in the Judeo-Christian tradition and those who oppose those traditional values. The public debate and the rancor over some of the more controversial issues is heated and in some cases violent. As a result, teachers are "gun-shy" about what can be taught in the name of "character education."

The roaring controversy about prayer in school has been a lightning rod issue for decades in our public schools. Those who oppose prayer in school have voraciously attacked any form of religious influence in public education. As a result, school administrators and teachers have become fearful of any activity that might be interpreted as "religious." The fear of legal action and political intimidation has produced a public education policy in many schools that is reluctant to teach anything that makes a value judgment about morality and issues of right and wrong. There are many varying opinions about whose standards of right and wrong should be adopted and taught. Most people do not object to the idea of teaching values in schools. The conflict begins when trying to decide whose values should be taught.

If you listen to the most vocal political voices, you get the impression that any mention of values or absolutes that might be attributed to "God" would be equal to some form of sinister mind control. Such brainwashing would violate the right of children to reach their own conclusions on such matters. Well, all I can say is that sometimes brains need some washing, and I believe our schools must play a significant role in the process. I believe that even though parental apathy seems to be very high, most parents want an educational system that will effectively prepare their children to be successful in life. I also believe that character education has to be supported by parents, teachers, school administrators and the public. And, I believe evidence exists that character education would be embraced by most Americans if it were properly presented. The fact is, the vast majority of Americans still believe in God.

In an age that seems to deny religion and God at every turn, the fact remains that most Americans still exercise personal faith. For instance, take a look at the following poll that determined public views and practices about our Thanksgiving holiday.

•

Poll: Findings on God and Thanksgiving

Scripps Howard News Service
November 14, 2000

"Do you and your family usually have a special gathering for a meal at Thanksgiving?"

Yes 92%
No 8%

"Do you normally say a special grace of thanksgiving at this meal?"

Yes 83%
No 17%

"This is a tough question, but give me your best answer. Do you think God has given special blessings to the United States?"

Yes 62%
No 33%
Don't Know 5%

"Did God help America become a free and secure nation?"

Yes 65%
No 28%
Don't Know 7%

(Source: Survey of 1,005 adult residents of the United States interviewed by telephone from Oct. 15-27 in a poll sponsored by Scripps Howard News Service and the E.W. Scripps School of Journalism at Ohio University.)

•

The results of this poll indicate the majority of Americans not only practice giving thanks to God, but they also believe that God took an active role in American history and gave special blessings to our country. If this poll is an accurate reflection of American opinion, and I believe it is, why would we think that Americans would not eagerly support character education curriculum in our public schools—even if some of the moral principles are attributed to God? I'm not advocating the teaching of specific religion in public schools, but there are certain basic values that originated in the Judeo-Christian heritage I believe should be taught to our children. These Judeo-Christian values, which are missing from our schools, are the absolutes and truths to which Cal Thomas referred. These are the core values that produced an educated, responsible succession of productive, successful Americans for over 200 years.

I don't want to engage in a debate about teaching religion in public schools. I want to make a strong case for the teaching of character. That should be acceptable to people of all faiths. Is there anyone who would seriously oppose the teaching of honesty in our schools?

Our children need to understand the full effect the issue of honesty will have upon their entire lives. They need to be shown and taught that honesty is the basic building block of all human relationships.

chapter five

Accepting Responsibility

It's no secret that accepting responsibility—one of the greatest characteristics of Americans—has been severely undermined. We have become a nation populated by large numbers of people who do not want to accept responsibility for their own actions. Our ancestors would roll over in their graves at some of the ideas we have come to regard as acceptable responses to difficulty and adversity.

I believe there are many people in America who really believe they somehow have an inalienable right to go through life and never experience problems that can't be blamed on others. Now, you might say, "Bob...don't you think people have always tried to blame other people for their problems?" I would answer that question by saying yes.

People have always tried to blame others for problems. I don't deny that it is a human characteristic to deny problems. What I am talking about here is the ridiculous number of things people in our day seem to think they have no responsibility for.

For instance, American lawyers have contributed to a common public hope that civil litigation might produce a personal, financial windfall. If you feel you have been inconvenienced —sue somebody! If you feel you have been discriminated against—sue somebody! If you feel someone received something you should have received —sue somebody! If you can sue somebody, the possibility exists that a bunch of money might fall into your bank account.

Fortunately, the truth is that the law and our courts are still based in fact and truth. Truly ridiculous judgements are not that common. However, when a huge financial judgement is granted to a victim who filed a seemingly ridiculous suit, it gets a lot of publicity. The truth is that far more lawsuits are finalized out of court than eventually go to a full trial. In other words, the parties reach a mutual settlement. Because there is such prohibitive cost involved in defending a lawsuit, many people and companies will agree to a financial settlement even if they feel they have done nothing wrong. It's just cheaper to pay something to settle a matter than to go through the horrendous expense of a lengthy legal fight.

What does all this have to do with accepting responsibility? I think a lot. The fact that many people receive financial rewards merely by filing or threatening to file a lawsuit has created a public perception that there is money waiting at the courthouse if you can just manage to be abused in some way. The news media gives litigation a lot of publicity and our children see it and hear it. There is truly an atmosphere that pervades our society that we are all victims of some kind. A victim's group exists for every possible injustice and many seek retribution in the courts. In the case of our schools, one of the main concerns of teachers and administrators is that they will be sued by the parents of the children they are trying to teach. In fact, it is not unusual for students to threaten their teachers with legal action for some perceived injustice. Sadly, injustice can be interpreted in a teacher's attempt to make a student responsible for his or her own actions.

Accepting responsibility for our actions is one of the most important qualities we can have. If you or I refuse to recognize our mistakes, there is no possibility that we can improve and grow. If you or I seek to blame others for our disappointments, we will become bitter and disillusioned with life and with our own ability to be successful. After all, if others have the power to keep us "down," then how can we possibly get "up?" Well, in countries where freedom and economic prosperity are restricted, people might be legitimately prohibited from doing and being what they want to be. This is NOT true for Americans. We live in a free society and have the unlimited ability to be as successful as we can be IF we realize that the possibility of being successful depends on our own actions. This means we also have to accept responsibility for our difficulties and our failures.

When people can accept their role in failure or disappointment or for problem behaviors (excessive alcohol use, taking drugs, dishonesty, etc.), they have the ability to overcome those problems and improve their future. If they deny the problems are a result of their own action and persist in blaming their difficulties on others, they will be forever mired in misery, self-pity and continued disappointment.

Les Brown is one of the finest motivational speakers in the world and he said something about accepting responsibility that goes to the heart of the issue: *"If you take responsibility for yourself you will develop a hunger to accomplish your dreams."* Isn't the main objective of education to prepare young people to be the best they can be?

Being the best we can be requires having a vision that we can be more than we are at the moment. Being the best we can be requires improvement and personal growth. Improvement and growth require hard work, determination and perseverance. At the root of these qualities is the ability and the willingness to take responsibility for our own actions. If we are unwilling to do that, we will have no dreams and we will not have the tools to grow.

Another critical element of accepting responsibility was provided by former First Lady Eleanor Roosevelt who said: *"In the long run, we shape our lives, and we shape ourselves. The process never ends until we die. And the choices we make are ultimately our own responsibility."* Much is being said in society today about the need to make good choices, but I don't hear good choice making linked to personal responsibility as directly as Mrs. Roosevelt tied them together. Think about it. Making a good choice requires honesty and it requires an honest look at the things for which we are responsible and accountable. Being the best we can be requires, as Mrs. Roosevelt said, that we shape ourselves and our lives for as long as we live. It is a process that is driven by good and bad choices, and the ability to make good choices is our willingness to be responsible for our own actions.

Another great American, Abraham Lincoln, said: *"You cannot escape the responsibility of tomorrow by evading it today."* I think this makes a huge point about the negative aspect of refusing to accept responsibility. The truth is that all we try to escape today will probably come around to haunt us tomorrow. The biblical truth that we "reap what we sow" applies here. It makes no difference how we attempt to deny our responsibility. If we have responsibility for something and we deny it, our denial will merely prolong the agony of whatever problem we are denying.

Finally, noted author M. Scott Peck had this to say: *"Whenever we seek to avoid the responsibility for our own behavior, we do so by attempting to give that responsibility to some other individual or organization or entity. But this means we then give away our power to that entity."* If we make others responsible for our success or our failure we truly lose the attitude that success requires. To be successful, people must believe they have the power to shape their own lives and that they will benefit from their efforts. If that idea is lost, the likelihood of a person maximizing his potential becomes very unlikely.

Excuses

How is the unwillingness to accept responsibility demonstrated? Most frequently it appears as an excuse. As a matter of fact, whenever you hear someone making an excuse, that person is usually evading personal responsibility in one way or another. I'm not saying there are not instances when we have a good excuse for something. I'm saying that there is usually more to the story, and it's in the "more to the story" part that avoiding responsibility can be found. For example, if I am 30 minutes late for a meeting, my excuse might be the heavy traffic. Well, it may be that I did hit some traffic, but the real reason I was late was that I didn't leave early enough for the meeting. An excuse may have a tinge of truth in it, but it covers for some behavioral fact.

When we fall into the habit of making excuses, we are doing huge harm to ourselves and are keeping ourselves from being successful. How does an excuse hinder success? Well, whenever we make an excuse and repeat it often enough, we come to believe it as the truth. When we accept things as being truthful, they become the basis for the things we do or do not do. If we believe our own excuses, we will eventually excuse ourselves right out of the door of success and achievement. The excuse will have more power in our lives than our own will.

How can children and young people become successful and be all they can be if they do not learn the importance of accepting responsibility for their own actions? How can they learn how to accept responsibility unless they are taught how to do so? The earlier a child begins to learn the importance of taking responsibility, the better off he will be in life. For this reason it is critically important for students to learn this vital skill and embrace this quality. I believe parents must help schools teach this critical skill in the classroom. Young people must understand the direct connection between accepting responsibility and their future success.

In our family we do this in an unusual way, but we are hopeful we will see the fruits of our labor in the years to come. As I mentioned earlier we have four children—Britton, Brad, Ashley and Stephanie. We have tried to get our children to think more about their responsibilities in life than their rights. I don't know about you, but I really get annoyed when I hear people constantly tell others what they have a right to do or say. I realize in a free society we are guaranteed certain rights. I am grateful. But I also know that my rights end where the rights of others begin. For example, I know people have a right to smoke, but their right to do so ends at my nose! I realize people have a right to swear, but not in front of my wife or children. I believe what little ears shouldn't hear, big mouths shouldn't say. So with that said, we have taken a little bit of liberty with our U.S. Constitution in our family and changed the focus from a Bill of Rights to a Bill of Responsibilities.

In part it reads, "We the members of the Alexander family, in order to form a more responsible family, establish justice, insure domestic tranquility, provide for the common defense, promote the general welfare, and secure the blessings of liberty to ourselves and our posterity, do ordain and establish the Constitution for the Alexander family. Our Bill of Responsibilities includes the following:

1) We have a responsibility to always tell the truth.
2) We have a responsibility to be honest and trustworthy.
3) We have a responsibility to be responsible.
4) We have a responsibility to respect others and ourselves.
5) We have a responsibility to display good manners.
6) We have a responsibility to be loyal.
7) We have a responsibility to be helpful.

8) We have a responsibility to be friendly and kind.

9) We have a responsibility to be obedient.

10) We have a responsibility to be pleasant and cheerful.

11) We have a responsibility to be courteous.

12) We have a responsibility to be strong and brave.

13) We have a responsibility to do our chores.

14) We have a responsibility to be thrifty.

15) We have a responsibility to honor God in everything we do.

If all parents and adults would teach their children a Bill of Responsibilities along with the Bill of Rights, our land would be blessed with the results of that kind of instruction. Can you imagine the improved attitudes and behavior children would have when they arrive at school? What if schools were to begin teaching the same Bill of Responsibilities? What if businesses started teaching the same thing? If this did happen, there is no question that our nation would be a better and greater place to live.

chapter six

Respecting Others

The third key in character education that is vital to the success of young people involves learning the importance of respect. I find it sad and disheartening to see how principles of respect have been so eroded in American culture. The principle of respect is foundational to the American experience because we are a nation of laws. I've begun this chapter making this point because there is no doubt that respect for the law is diminishing, particularly among younger people. Respect for the law is the safety net of our republic and if that is lost, our country and our society are in for some tough sledding.

I believe that a lack of respect for the law begins with a lack of respect for other concepts and principles. As those other concepts and principles lose respect, the cancer moves closer to the safety net. If the safety net fails, the potential for chaos exists. Can you imagine living in an America where the law is completely ignored and is unenforceable? Well, I can't imagine it either and I don't want to experience such a condition. Respect for law begins with self-respect and with respect for the rights of others. As self-respect diminishes, respect for others dwindles. When we lose respect for others, we put our feet on a slippery slope that ends in selfishness and misery.

The singular issue of respect may be the most serious problem facing our nation today. There are just so many things that no longer command the respect they deserve and I want to discuss some of the more important items. Before I do, it is only fair to say that I am what you would consider a social conservative. I was raised in a family that taught me the difference between right and wrong. I was taught that there are absolutes and that some things are just not appropriate and should not be done. I was taught that the moral health of our society depends on people behaving in as decent and proper a manner as possible. I was taught that there are basic standards of honesty and propriety that every responsible human being should follow and support. One of these standards or principles involves being respectful of certain things and people—not because of WHO they are—because of WHAT they are.

In my view there are three major categories of respect that must be understood. The three categories are:

1) Respect for authority
2) Respect for property
3) Respect for self and others

Respect for Authority

While I certainly agree that people have to earn respect, I don't believe earning respect is the only justification for being respectful. That, I think, is one of the major flaws in current attitudes. An example of why this is a problem can be

> I grew up to always respect authority and respect those in charge.
>
> —Grant Hill (NBA Player)

found right in our school classrooms. Teachers should be respected because they are teachers. Regardless of their personalities and individual quirks, teachers are placed in a position of responsibility by education authorities and as such are entitled to the respect of their students. Do you see the difference I'm talking about? Teachers are worthy of two forms of respect. One form is for the position they hold. The other is for them as individuals. A teacher may be respected for his position as a teacher and forfeit respect for his ability to teach based on his ability. However, even though a teacher may not be respected for his teaching ability, he would still be entitled to respect for holding the position as a teacher. What I'm talking about is a basic respect for authority. How Americans have come to be less than respectful of authority can be hotly debated, but the fact remains that it has happened and it threatens the very fabric of our nation. As I was growing up I was taught by my parents to respect authority. I respected my teachers because they were my teachers. I respected police officers because they were police officers. I respected elected officials because they were chosen to lead by the people who voted for them. I was not told I had to like people in authority, but I was taught they should be respected by virtue of their positions of authority.

Our society has become more and more informal over the years. Children today are allowed to address adults by their first name, rather than by Mr. or Mrs. How many times have you heard adults themselves say to a child "Oh, just call me Bob"? This may seem like a small thing but it detracts from the adult's position of authority over that child. It makes the child and the adult equal in the child's mind. When I was growing up, I would have been chastised severely if I had called an adult by his first name, even if the adult invited me to do so. Standards and values erode over a long period of time and the erosion begins with seemingly small things that are "no big deal." Well, the specific thing might not seem to be a big deal but the underlying principle may be huge. That is the case in the example of a child addressing an adult by first name.

The underlying principle here involves the respect that children have for adults merely because they are adults. When a child is required to address an adult as Mr. or Mrs., it sends a subtle message that the adult has some sort of implied authority over the child. The child is not equal to the adult in age, experience, or maturity, and the child should recognize that fact. When all adults become Bob, Jim, Betty, or Jane to the child, the idea of authority begins to be removed. When you have a generation of young people who have been allowed to treat adults as equals, you end up with a society that has difficulty respecting any authority figure.

Now that I've opened up this can of worms, you may be thinking, "Bob, I agree with the principle of what you are saying but there are a lot of sick adults out there and our children need to be on guard about trusting strangers and others who might do them harm." I understand that there are some bad people out there and I understand that children have to use some judgment in the things they do. I believe it is not that difficult to teach children the concept of respect for authority and also give them tools to protect themselves from abusive authority. However, I have a big problem with throwing out the concept of respect for authority because there may be a few potential problems and some bad apples in the barrel. Authority must be respected as a principle and honored simply because it exists. Authority is one of the primary foundations of stability for our society as a whole.

I hope you understand what I'm saying about respect for authority and, more important, I hope you will also understand that some common sense needs to be applied to the discussion. I realize that authority can be abusive and inappropriate. I realize that there have been many instances of people in authority using their positions to victimize young people. When I advocate respect for authority, I am not saying that all other forms of intelligence should be abandoned. Obviously, children need to be taught to respect authority, but they also need to understand that a small number of people can't be completely trusted. In that regard, children need to be educated about appropriate and inappropriate behavior.

The benefits of learning to respect authority far outweigh possible negatives. When young people learn to accept and respect authority, they have a better chance of being successful throughout their lives. Have you ever heard of an employer actively seeking people who resist authority, direction, and control? I hardly think so. When children learn to respect authority, they are better citizens, better professionals, and better parents! Respect for authority is also something outstanding leaders have to understand, because before they can lead, they have to learn to follow.

Ultimately, respect for authority helps build a certain amount of personal self-discipline in children. Showing respect for authority represents a conscious, voluntary act. It is a matter of making a choice to control the self-will and surrender it to a form of authority. It is the opposite of rebellion and requires the development of patience and self-control.

Respect for Property

The next category of respect to consider involves respect for the property of others. Property can be publicly or privately owned. The point is that property not owned by me is owned by someone else and it does not belong to me! The owner of the property is entitled to decide how that property will be used and I do not have the right to trespass, use, or change it. Neither do I have the right to steal it, damage it, or vandalize it. It's not mine!

In the United States of America our personal freedoms include the right to privately own property. Property can be a piece of land or any other item. Private ownership of property is one of the basic foundations of personal freedom and respect of that right is key to preserving not only our freedom but also the stability of our society. Freedom only exists where there is complete respect for rights of property ownership. Whenever you or I have the opportunity to visit another person's home or business, we are bound by the rules of conduct the other person may have established. If they do not permit smoking, then we shouldn't smoke. If they require shirts and shoes to be worn, we should wear shirts and shoes. Americans are free to protect their property as they see fit as long as they do not violate the law.

Respect for private and public property is an indication and a reflection of a person's character. If a person does not respect the property of others, it demonstrates something is missing in their concept of what is right and what is wrong. Children and young people frequently do things that demonstrate a lack of respect for the property of others and it is because they have not been taught the importance of this principle. Vandalism is usually committed by adolescent males. Adults rarely engage in vandalism. I think most vandals commit their acts because they think what they are doing is funny or comical. In other situations, vandalism is committed out of revenge for some perceived injustice. Whatever the reason for vandalism, the truth is that it is a stupid act and demonstrates a total lack of respect for the property of others. It is also cruel. Vandalism always creates a personal financial loss of some magnitude for the victims. If the vandals damage private property, the loss is personal to the property owner. If the vandals damage public property, the loss is shared by the community in the form of higher taxes and usage fees. Vandalism is not funny and young people must be taught the truth of this.

The other primary form of disrespect for property involves theft. I like to use a fairly broad definition of theft and say that theft has occurred when a person takes or exercises control of property that belongs to another without the owner's permission. This means that theft can include "borrowing" items and not returning them. It also means that theft can involve downloading intellectual property from the Internet, or the unauthorized copying of computer programs. With respect to young people, the theft of intellectual property is the newest and most widespread form of theft in the world.

In our digital world, the theft of intellectual property is also practiced by large numbers of adults and their children see them doing it. The advent of computers and the digital processing of information and data have made it extremely easy for anyone to acquire property of this kind. Many people are ignoring the fact they are stealing when they download something from the Internet (music, books, articles, etc.). When a computer is copying something to a disk, it just doesn't seem as if theft is happening. After all, the original copy still exists and nobody will miss or even know that it has been copied illegally. We must remember that just because something is easy does not make it morally right and that is what we should be teaching our young people.

Theft is theft by any name and the cost of theft is high to both victim and thief. People who are victims of theft experience damage and direct financial losses. If the theft victim is a business, the theft eventually translates into higher costs for consumers. As far as the thieves are concerned, they are likely to suffer incarceration and social rejection. No thief has much hope for a meaningful, productive life. Even when a thief has "paid his debt to society" by going to prison, he is scarred for life as a thief. The opportunities for meaningful employment or positions of trust are severely diminished.

Respect for Self and Others

Finally, the third foundation of respect involves respect for self and for others. I think it quite simply boils down to one major idea: If we can't get along with ourselves, we will have difficulty getting along with others. This idea isn't new with me. I picked up the principle from The Golden Rule: "Do unto others as you would have them do unto you." You would think this would be a simple and easy thing to understand and do.

It sounds like common sense. Years ago, it probably was. But I have come to believe that common sense is not always common practice. I see it every day and I bet you do, too. Today, when you realize what young people are doing to themselves, it's pretty clear that there may be something missing in their thought patterns. Adolescent use of alcohol, drugs, body piercing and tattooing are taking place at an unprecedented rate. People do things because they have come to believe the things they do are acceptable. When unacceptable behavior becomes acceptable, reason and logic begin to be distorted. Unfortunately, the ability to understand and practice The Golden Rule becomes distorted as well.

The Golden Rule is best understood by the idea of only treating others as we are willing to be treated. I think the key word here is *willing*. First, you have to imagine yourself in someone else's place in any given circumstance and then you have to decide if you would be willing to be treated as you are treating them. If the answer is no, then you are violating the rule. Whenever we violate The Golden Rule, we are actually practicing unfairness, hypocrisy, and living by a double standard. What is good for me is not good for you! I believe the unwillingness to practice The Golden Rule is the result of a lack of basic respect for others. It's almost like denying the truth of their feelings and their human dignity. To be capable of giving that kind of empathy and respect to others, the first requirement is respect for yourself. If we don't respect ourselves, we won't respect others. When we violate The Golden Rule, we are displaying a lack of concern that is foundational for basic morality.

chapter seven

Teaching Character

The concept of teaching character education is not something most people disagree with. The disagreement begins when you start getting into the details of what constitutes character education. Just exactly whose values should be taught and how should principles of character be presented? What are the desired results of character education? On the surface it seems that character education should be a simple matter. Obviously, the three issues I have presented in this book should have no opposition. Who could protest teaching honesty, accepting responsibility, and respect? Few would argue against these principles in their basic meanings. The fight starts when you start trying to define these terms in a political and social sense.

Unfortunately, the subject of character education is rife with politics. The liberal left is on guard against any form of character education that might involve God or other training that reinforces "traditional morality." The conservative right argues that any character-based education program should embrace the tenets of biblical wisdom about right and wrong. The liberal left believes that conservative, biblical approaches to character education are designed to drill students in certain types of behavior and get them in lock-step. They believe that this kind of teaching uses techniques of "indoctrination" to produce behavioral results that support a conservative world view. In plain English, liberals don't want any form of character education that teaches absolute conditions of right and wrong. They specifically oppose any programs that undermine the ideas of group sensitivity, diversity, and situational ethics. For example, any character-based curriculum that might lead students to oppose abortion or make negative value judgments about "alternative lifestyles" will be opposed by the liberal left.

In case you are wondering where I stand in this debate, let me clear up any doubt. I mentioned earlier that I am a conservative, and I believe that character education by definition involves teaching biblical principles. However, I do not believe that the goal of character education is solely to change behavior. I believe the overall goal of education is to prepare students to be more successful in life! Part of the preparation for being successful in life involves teaching technical academic skills. Another part of education involves teaching children how to be successful as human beings. Successful people have to know how to read and write and they also need to understand how honesty, accepting responsibility, and respect for others will impact their future. After they understand the importance of these qualities, they can begin to make behavioral choices consistent with those qualities. The point is that behavior follows the choices people make and choices are driven by the things they believe to be true.

For character education to be successful, it must impact the student and the level of core belief. Any character curriculum that falls short of impacting core beliefs will not produce long-term, sustained changes in character. Some say a person's character is defined by what he does and not by what he says or believes. I say that our character is determined by the things we believe, and the things we believe drive our behavior. If I believe it is OK to steal, I will steal. If I believe it is OK to lie, I will lie.

Good character requires doing the right thing, even when it is fearful. For that to happen, a person must first know what the right thing IS! Secondly, they have to believe that doing the right thing is more important than any temporary discomfort they may experience as a result of doing the right thing. People must believe that successful human relationships are built on trust and being able to depend on our fellow human beings to do the right thing. Students need to understand and believe that people who do the right things over a long period of time can expect a higher level of success than people who choose to do the wrong things.

Consider this scenario. Liz and Paula both work in the same office and they have similar duties. However, there are some significant differences between the two. Liz has more work experience than Paula. Liz also has more educational credentials than Paula. A higher paying job has just become vacant and Liz and Paula are the prime contenders for the position. Who will get the promotion?

If the promotion decision is to be made solely on the basis of experience and education, Liz wins the new job. However, we all know that more is involved in these kinds of decisions. The more that is involved is the character of the candidates. The rest of this story is that Liz is always 15 minutes late to every meeting she attends and rarely turns in her assignments when they are due. The technical quality of her work is excellent, but it's always late. Liz also tends to shade the truth about things and she isn't fully trusted by her peers. Finally, Liz complains a lot and gossips about other people as if she might get a reward for it.

Paula, on the other hand is always on time, dependable and cheerful. She can always be depended on to tell the truth and she does whatever she can to help everyone on her team be more productive and successful. Now, who do you think will get the promotion? Paula, of course! And Paula will get the promotion because of her character, not her technical ability.

The differences between Liz and Paula go deeper than their behavior. The real differences are found in the things they believe about themselves and other people. Liz, for example, believes that she is special and a little bit smarter than others. Liz believes her opinions and her insight are so unique that being on time is not important. The fact that others may be inconvenienced by her poor planning is not important to her. She believes she has other qualities that offset her tardiness.

Paula, on the other hand, believes that other people's time is as important as hers and she believes being on time is important. Paula also believes that she is just one person on a team and that everyone needs to contribute and pull their weight if the team is to be successful. Paula believes that the most important thing she has is her word and is therefore rigorously honest in all that she does.

The story of Liz and Paula is repeated countless times each year in companies, organizations, and groups all over the world. People who are dependable and can be counted on get the promotions. People who are undependable are passed over. The difference is found in their character and their character is driven by the things they believe.

I think this hypothetical story makes the point about the relationship of belief and behavior. Paula got the promotion based on her behavior, but her behavior was the result of what she believed. So, if we hope to provide character education in our schools, it must be of a type that will change behavior by changing beliefs. When we can impact belief, change becomes voluntary and authentic. When change is voluntary and authentic, it will change the lives of people in a dynamic way. Regardless of how much the liberal left will protest against it, character is a function of morality, and education has a twin goal: The intellectual and the moral development of the pupil. I hope you agree with me about what needs to be taught to our young people. The next issue to discuss is how to teach it. The balance of this book is devoted to that subject.

chapter eight

Before and After

A review of the results proves that when students are taught the principles mentioned earlier in this book, their academic and personal lives are tremendously enhanced. Their grades improve, their relationships improve, and they are happier individuals. When students know what's expected of them as people—how to behave, how to stretch and grow—they deliver. Our young people didn't start out in life trying to be disagreeable, dishonest, or to shirk responsibility. They weren't born with a bad attitude toward authority; they learned it and they can unlearn it.

I've personally had the privilege of helping many schools implement a character-based program called the I CAN program. It was designed by The Zig Ziglar Corporation to help students improve their outlook on life and to give them a solid foundation on which to build a satisfying, secure future.

I'm using the I CAN program as the best example of what a character-based program can do for students because it incorporates every essential ingredient needed for successful living. The foundation stones of the program are honesty, integrity, character, love, faith and loyalty. Curriculum material deals with achieving good relationships with family, classmates, and employers; developing a healthy self-image; setting and reaching goals; obtaining and maintaining a good attitude; avoiding bad habits and curing bad habits that are already in place. The program also teaches patriotism and the Free Enterprise System, topics that are particularly relevant in light of the terrorist attacks of September 11, 2001. For the first time in our school-age children's generation, there is a true uncertainty of the future. None of us knows where this war on terrorism is going to take us or how long it will last. Now, more than ever before, young people need to know and understand what they believe in, what they are living for, and how to live without fear and anxiety. When the proper foundation is in place, students are empowered. They feel more in control of their lives and the uncertainty of our future as a nation does not chip away at their purpose for living.

In all of my years of involvement in our country's educational system, the need for a program that instructs students on the foundational issues of living has never been more apparent. Students enrolled in the I CAN program learn how to identify and obtain through a plan of action what they want in life. They are also shown how to overcome a poor self-image and how to achieve and maintain a positive mental attitude. Goal setting and how to reach those goals once they are set is perhaps the section of the program that gives students the most hope for their future. The program teaches the philosophy that you can have everything in life you want if you will just help enough other people get what they want. When students engage this principle, it changes their lives and prepares them for a tremendous future.

Time and time again test and survey results show that students who adopt the traits of honesty, respect, and accepting responsibility excel. The specific examples I'm about to use are only a handful of the results I have on file. But for space limitations I'd mention every school and teacher involved because I'm as proud for them as they are of their students.

Before I get into statistics and test results, I think it best that you hear from some of the students who have participated in the I CAN program. Dr. Angela Rasmussen, who has worked extensively with the Hillsborough County school system in Florida to get businesses and the community at large to support implementation of "The I Can Course," sent me the following letters.

The first is from Amber and she titled it, "'I Can' Way of Life."

Ever since I learned about "I Can," my life has improved for the better. I'm making good grades (I'm on the high honor roll), I'm motivated to do good stuff, and I'm an overall better person. Since I've learned about "I Can," I've discovered respect, love, optimism, honesty, and character. This is but a small sample of all that I've learned in "I Can." "I Can" is one of the best things that ever happened to me. I feel like I can do anything and it's a great feeling. I wish everyone could feel as great and terrific as I do. It's wonderful to live for the love of life. Every day I give myself a "check up from the neck up" so I can be the best person I can be.

Elicia wrote: *The "I Can" program has helped me in so many ways. One important way that it has helped is that I am now trying to set goals and getting my act together. In the summer I felt that I was not going to make it, but I realized that there are going to be hard times and I have just got to move on and get the "winner's attitude." I knew that attitude was in me all the time.*

Even though I already had the ability in me, this "I Can" program has brought my good attitude to my attention. Now that my self-esteem and self-respect have been developed, I am making all A's and I have been winning many events. I won first place in the school multicultural contest, I was written about in the paper, and now I have been chosen for "Climbing to the Top."

Student Heather Marie wrote a good overview of what she thinks the I CAN program is all about and how it has helped her. She writes:

The "I Can" material is built on a philosophy that will help see you to the top. It helps you build a solid foundation for life. Positive thinking is one of the many things "I Can" teaches us. Positive thinking is the optimistic hope that you can accomplish other seemingly impossible tasks. I thought it was impossible to make the honor roll but positive thinking has changed my thoughts. I have accomplished what I thought was once impossible. I have achieved my goal. I made the honor roll. I owe it all to the "I Can" material. In the "I Can" material it also teaches loyalty, trust, honesty, and many more wonderful things to get us through life. "I Can" is the positive way to go.

In March of 1993, Jeanette and Jennifer, both students at Genesis High School in Bastrop, Texas, wrote letters of thanks to Zig Ziglar. Let's see what Jeanette had to say:

...First of all I want to thank you for letting me have one of the greatest opportunities in my life. With the "I Can" Program added to my ability, I have learned that I can do anything that I want to do as well as be anyone that I wish to be. As I was growing up I was always being told that I was dumb and stupid and was never going to get anywhere in life. But all that changed when I began taking this course. My teacher has taught me a great deal and now I am convinced that I am a winner. Not only has my life changed but the way I see and feel about myself and others has changed as well. Once again, thank you for this great opportunity and you will soon see me at the top.

Here's what Jennifer wrote: *I am writing to say "Thank You" for enlightening my life with your wonderful knowledge of people and how I can suc-*

ceed in life. You have helped me change my way of thinking and you have encouraged me to do the very best at everything I do. I do not seem to snap back at people the way I used to. I can see my attitude changing daily. Once again, I would like to say "THANK YOU" from the bottom of my heart.

Teachers Have Their Say, Too!

In a March 23, 1998, letter, Charlene Garrett, a Reading Resource Specialist from Dowdell Junior High School (Hillsborough County Public Schools) in Tampa, Florida, wrote in part: … *I am so proud that we will begin a fourth year of the "I Can" curriculum. This coming week our school will take the Stanford Achievement Test (SAT). As I am thinking about the upcoming week, I know our school will again be an academic success story. Just to show you how confident I am, please take a moment and read about our successes with the Stanford Achievement Test.*

In 1996, at the end of my school's first year completing the "I Can" curriculum, my school had a 12 percentage point increase in our school-wide reading score on the SAT. During the second year (1997) using the "I Can" curriculum, our school increased 20 percentage points in our school-wide reading SAT score. I also did some research in other areas of our school and discovered a 4 percentage point increase in our state writing test scores, and our school had an 11 percentage point increase in our school-wide SAT mathematics score.

The standardized test scores just reinforced the research that I conducted at our school. As I've tracked our students, I can see the continued increase in academic achievement. Just look at (the following) statistics of students who have been involved with the curriculum for a two-year period.

Second Year "I Can" Students:

- *86.7 % increase in reading using Test Ready reading pre-test and post-test scores.*

- *57.14 % increased or had no change in attendance. Score based on targeted students.*

- *70.27 % decreased or had no change in discipline referrals. Score based on targeted students.*

- *75 % increased conduct grades. Score based on targeted students.*

Ms. Garrett continued, *"I know that standardized scores are important, but let me brag on other aspects of our "I Can" school. In our last year as a junior high school (1996), we were the district's foot-*

ball champions. We had our fist yearbook in the 34 year history of our school. We had over 90% of our students in clubs - a 60 % increase in club involvement for our school - and suspensions were down 33 percent. This was the year that over 80 % of our teachers knew that they would not be able to stay at our school, but the "I Can" curriculum gave them the confidence and the self-esteem to lead a multi-cultural, poor, inner-city school to the top. We were featured on a major TV news program as a "SUPER SCHOOL."

Now we are in our second year as a middle/magnet school with a new faculty who teach half in a traditional school and half in an environmental magnet school. Other schools in our district with similar divisions are having major problems but not our school. Recently a county visitor asked to have a major retreat at our school because she said, "I feel a spiritual presence at your school." I know what she means. You can visit our school to see our "I Can" Intramural banners, to read our displayed "I Can" students' and teachers' poetry, to watch our "I Can" TV morning show, take part in one of our "I Can" contests, or to just walk down the nature trail and stop a minute by our "I Can" butterfly garden. Our teachers, our students, and our administration have the "I Can" attitude, and we know we are making a difference. Finally, let me just say you and the "I

*Can" curriculum do make a difference in our stu-
dents' and our teachers' lives.*

I want to add that Charlene Garrett really does
have a lot to be excited about. Her school is not
attended by Tampa's wealthiest residents. On the
contrary, of the 909 students enrolled in the 1998-
99 school year, 558, or 61%, were on the free or
reduced price lunch. With so many transient
workers drawn to the harvesting of citrus and
other Florida crops, those figures are not at all surprising. What is surprising is seeing how quickly
the seeds of hope begin to sprout in "I CAN" students who come from these underprivileged
backgrounds.

Ms. Garrett provided me with some truly
remarkable numbers. During the 1997-98 school
year, there were 1,439 referrals, including bus
referrals. During the 1998-99 school year, referrals
dropped to 945—a 21% decrease in referrals—or
you could say the numbers reflect a 21% improvement in student behavior! Attendance also
improved over 3% for the same period of time.
The starting place for learning in a school environment is attendance. The capacity to learn
begins with good behavior. When those two
things are in place, an attitude of hope propels students to new academic heights.

Even Ex-Students Have Opinions

Jessica, an ex-student of Gateway High School in Clovis, California, contacted her old school in hopes of obtaining I CAN course material for her personal use. When she learned the course had been discontinued, she felt strongly that it was a mistake and wrote a letter to the school explaining her reasoning. In part, here is what she wrote:

It has come to my attention that Gateway High School is no longer offering the "I Can" course.

When I was attending Gateway during the years of 1987-1989, I was experiencing many emotional problems. One of my teachers, Ms. Mahoney, suggested that I look into a course that would help me look at my life in a more positive and optimistic manner. This was the "I Can" course and I believe it helped me through a very difficult time.

In these three "I Can" classes that were being offered, we learned how to look at life more positively and how to get along better with other people. We learned many new skills for success, such as: goal setting, communication, and understanding others' feelings. We were constantly provided opportunities to stretch, grow, and build our self-confidence.

Many of us were negative, critical, and felt like losers, or in other words, had an "I Can't" attitude.

With a daily dose of the "I Can" course, we became more hopeful. I personally began to succeed. As the semester progressed, I began to try harder in school, to treat myself and others with more dignity and respect. I began reaching my goals. It was a life saver.

You might imagine my dismay when I learned that this fantastic course was no longer offered by Gateway High School. I can only urge you and/or whomever is responsible for the discontinuation of "I Can" to reconsider the offering of this program. I know it helped me, and I also know it can and did help others.

Thank you for taking the time for this plea.

Students, teachers, and even ex-students all have great things to say about the I CAN course. Nothing, however, tells the story of success better than factual statistics. From January through May 1993, the I CAN curriculum was taught as a semester long program in Region 2, Corpus Christi, Texas. Five school districts in South Texas taught 17 I CAN classes over the course of the semester, presenting pre-tests and post-tests to determine the percentage of change in the students' thinking. The results speak for themselves!

Question	Pre-test	Post-Test (Agree)	Point Change (Agree)	Percent Improvement
I should prepare for a job interview.				
	12.4%	75.2%	+62.8	+406.5%
My friends can change or influence the way I act or behave.				
	13.4%	54.7%	+41.3	+208.2%
Negative actions/attitudes decrease teamwork.				
	18.1%	66.5%	+48.4	+167.4%
Goals are reached by luck.				
	53.7%	23.1%	+30.6	+132.4%
People with negative attitudes can't be changed.				
	78.5%	25.7%	+52.8	+105.4%
Some people always seem happy.				
	25.2%	72.9%	+47.7	+89.3%
Positive affirmations can help me be successful.				
	23.8%	64.7%	+40.0	+71.8%
Helping others in my daily life helps me.				
	41.1%	68.2%	+27.1	+65.9%
Happiness and peace of mind can be a result of hard work.				
	33.8%	53.5%	+19.7	+58.3%
People can look at something that happens and react in either a positive or negative way.				
	43.1%	67.0%	+23.9	+55.5%
Positive actions/attitudes improve teamwork.				
	28.7%	70.4%	+41.7	+45.3%
I must like myself to be successful.				
	40.7%	56.4%	+15.7	+38.6%
I must work on my goals daily.				
	58.2%	78.3%	+20.1	+34.5%
Skills are learned.				
	53.0%	69.0%	+16.0	+30.2%
I can learn about myself by exploring my future.				
	51.1%	65.6%	+14.5	+28.4%

You can tell by reading the statements above that the I CAN Program is different from other courses in that it asks students to consider the responsibility they have for themselves. Perhaps for the first time, students are challenged to think beyond the moment and consider the long-term results of their present day decisions. I've witnessed how the understanding of this concept empowers young people. Those students who have been living in less than positive environments see a way to change their circumstances. They have hope for a better tomorrow.

A Dallas, Texas, high school instituted the I CAN Program and their hopes were realized. A. Maceo Smith High School was in danger of being closed down because a study showed they were "low performing." After a year of teaching the I CAN Program, TASS test scores showed an improvement in math of 11%, an improvement in reading of 5%, and an improvement in writing of 7%. Ninety percent of 10th graders passed the persuasive essay—a fact of which they are particularly proud. The year before I CAN was taught, 69 seniors didn't graduate; the year after I CAN was taught only 10 seniors didn't graduate, incredible results from a school attended by students with a high risk of dropping out. Today, A.

Maceo Smith High School is no longer a "low performing" school.

I CAN Survey

Positive Life Attitudes for America did a survey to discover the impact of the I CAN program on high school students. Sixteen high schools representing 1,044 students responded. The results of that survey are as follows:

- Eighty-five per cent (85%) reported the I CAN class to be more enjoyable than others.
- Eighty-two per cent (82%) reported regularly applying I CAN learning to their lives and 67% reported using the principles and skills daily.
- Eighty-five per cent (85%) of the students reported a commitment to using I CAN principles for personal improvement.
- Seventy-six per cent (76%) reported the I CAN class had affected their overall performance (i.e., school, extra-curricular, work, athletic, etc.).
- Eighty-six per cent (86%) of students reported having a better self-image and more self-confidence.

- Eighty-eight per cent (88%) reported having a more positive attitude.

- Thirty-three per cent (33%) reported the I CAN class had helped improve their school attendance (i.e., reduced tardiness and absenteeism), while 62% were satisfied with their previous school attendance.

- Forty-six per cent (46%) reported making better grades.

- Fifty-nine per cent (59%) reported having a better attitude about school.

- Eighty-three per cent (83%) of the students reported being more enthusiastic and hopeful about life.

- Seventy-nine per cent (79%) of the students reported learning more about how to set and work toward goals.

- Fifty-one per cent (51%) reported being happier.

- Fifty-five per cent (55%) of the students reported getting along better with teachers and employers, while 41% were satisfied with those relationships prior to the course.

- Fifty-seven per cent (57%) reported getting along better with peers, while 42% got along as well as before.

- Fifty-one per cent (51%) of the students reported getting along better with family members, while 39% got along as well as before.

- Sixty-three per cent (63%) of the I CAN students reported being more patient and self-disciplined.

- Thirty-one per cent (31%) of the students definitely understood that smoking tobacco leads to using drugs and 19% thought this may be so, while 39% did not believe smoking leads to using drugs.

- Seventeen per cent (17%) of the students that smoked tobacco reported quitting smoking and another 22% stated they were smoking much less than before. Forty-five percent (45%) said they had never smoked tobacco before, while 31% stayed the same as before.

- Twenty per cent (20%) of the students reported they were drinking much less than before, 34% said they had never used alcohol, 14% said they had quit drinking and 40% stayed the same as before.

- Twenty-eight (28%) of the students reported quitting using drugs and 18% stated they had cut down on the use of drugs. Sixty one per cent (61%) of the students said they never used drugs before.

- Forty per cent (40%) of the students reported arguing and fighting less.

- Fifty-three per cent (53%) of the students reported caring for property and things more than before.

- Forty-nine per cent (49%) of the students reported improving their looks and dress while 49% saw no difference.

- Fifty-six per cent (56%) of I CAN students reported improving their moral code.

- Fifty-seven per cent (57%) of students reported making better choices (decisions) while 38% saw no difference.

- Seventy-one per cent (71%) of the students believed they could communicate better.

- Sixty-eight per cent (68%) of the students reported being more kind and helpful.

- Fifty-eight per cent (58%) of students reported more appreciation and greater understanding of our free enterprise system while 28% saw no difference.

- Forty-four per cent (44%) of the I CAN students reported a greater appreciation for America while 39% saw no difference.

In April of 2001 I received a letter from teacher Phyllis Sheffield of Pearland, Texas. She has been exposed to the I CAN program long enough to see how circumstances like the ones reported on statistically above played out in real life for her students. She walked down memory lane for me, recounting how she came to be known as the "I Can Lady." She told me how her students loved the format of the class, how they wrote plays, made videos and even stitched an I CAN quilt. The I CAN workbooks became the students' treasure, so much so that even though it's been many years since she started teaching the program, Phyllis often runs into ex-students in places like Wal-Mart and the overwhelming majority tell her they still have their I CAN workbooks. Phyllis closed her letter by saying that the skills taught in the I CAN program are just as necessary as the 3-R's. She said her experience with the I CAN program proved to her that teachers really can make positive life changes in their students and she highly recommends the program for any educational setting.

Principals and Superintendents Count

It wouldn't seem right to conclude this chapter without hearing from a school principal and a school district superintendent. Principal Paul Jennings of the Grapevine Colleyville ISD in Texas wrote to me in April of 2001 and said:

Let me tell you about the impact the "I Can" program has had on many of our youngsters in this community. We distributed the materials to our teachers after a staff development workshop that you conducted. Immediately after the workshop the teachers began using the principles of the program in their day to day instruction. But the most salient discovery was what I saw in the hallways....the cafeteria....the gymnasium and the bus stop. I began to notice...as did many of my teachers...that the students were beginning to "live" by the principles of the "I Can" program. The fact that students began to discover that...they can have everything in life they want...if they help enough other folks get what they want...began to become a reality to them.

Being "nice" is a choice. To have a friend...you must be a friend. Your attitude in life...is the MOST important indicator of your future success. All of these attributes...and many more helped our youngsters get over the sometimes rocky road of ado-

lescence. We can thank you, Bob, for bringing these important issues to light. Please keep up the great job…and help us stay focused on the "big deals" of life!

Superintendent Frank Belcher* had this to say:

I am writing to share my experiences with the "I Can" program that I have been associated with for over 20 years. I am currently Superintendent of Schools of the Texline Independent School District in Texas. This year our school is teaching the "I Can" program to all of our K-12 students. Without a doubt, this program will turn out to be the best thing our school does for students, the reason being that the life principles that we are teaching will benefit our students in anything they choose to do.

The "I Can" program is not only benefiting our students but also our teachers. I have seen a marked difference in the attitudes of our teaching staff as well as our students. I firmly believe that people's attitudes at the beginning of a project determine the ultimate success of that program. Last school year when we were investigating the program we received copies of the Elementary and Secondary curriculum guides for our teachers to look over. As they examined the program their comments were that they wanted to start the program now and not wait until next year, and that "this program will help me more than the kids."

I am pleased to report that we are about to finish our first year in the program. It has turned out to be a huge success. There have been times that some of our students have resisted the program, but we were determined to stay with it and apply an "I Can" principle—"Success is a process, not an event." The "I Can" program affords opportunities to be very creative and to apply your school's own touch in the way you structure the instruction. Our school has developed an "I Can" Honor Roll where we recognize students that have displayed an "I Can" attitude throughout the year.

One of my goals for the students that go to our school is to give them an advantage, that when they finish at Texline they will have the skills they will need to compete anywhere. A major part of providing that advantage is what is taught in the "I Can" program. It is my belief that the way to combat the drug use and violence in schools is to provide students with a strong character base as opposed to scare tactics and statistics. When students have been taught the importance of setting goals, the emphasis should be on what you have to do to achieve those goals and what obstacles will you have to overcome. The "I Can" program does just that.

I would like to conclude with my favorite "I Can" story, a real life example of the influence the "I Can" course can have on a student. When I was teaching the "I Can" course at a middle school I also taught 6th grade social studies. Part of the "I Can" course was to periodically write "I Likes" for each student. "I Likes" were small pieces of paper where students would write a short encouraging note of why they liked the person, and I incorporated these "I Likes" in my social studies classes. We usually did them on Fridays. I had a 6th grade student who had been retained the previous year and I decided that he would be the first person who we would do an "I Like" for. This took place the second week of school and I never thought about it much after that. On the last day of school in May I was walking through the PE dressing room as the students were gathering their PE clothes. This 6th grade student dropped his notebook on the floor and as I was in the process of helping him I noticed the "I Like" slips. I said, "You still have these slips from the second week of school." He told me he kept them in his notebook and when he was having a bad day he would read them. This taught me a valuable lesson of the importance of something as simple as an "I Like" and the difference it can make in the life of a student.

I can assure you, just as the students and educators you've heard from in this chapter have, that the I CAN program is a character building, life changing program that has positively influenced those who've experienced it, students and teachers alike.

*Note: Frank Belcher is presently the superintendent of the Canadian Independent School District in Canadian, Texas. He has implemented the I CAN Program there and is seeing positive results in the attitudes and behavior of his students.

chapter nine

Corporate America and Education Unite

We don't have a tremendous educational problem in America. What we have is a tremendous societal problem in America. Every single morning, somewhere in the United States of America, a man and his wife take their child to school with the expectation that the teacher will instruct their child in reading, writing and arithmetic. Unfortunately, those children arrive with all of the effects of having lived in our society. They arrive with the effects of vandalism, violence and promiscuity. Students suffer from the effects of drugs and drug abuse, alcohol and alcohol abuse, and even the drug with the plug—television.

Prime time TV depicts vandalism, violence, rape, suicide, and murder; then when the youth of America go out and replicate what they see on TV, we see stories of their arrests on the evening news, and we wonder what happened to make a child do such a thing.

The fact of the matter is we're never going to teach the ABC's of education until we've taught the ABC's of life: ATTITUDE, BEHAVIOR and CHARACTER. Everyone agrees that these principles should be taught at home; everyone also recognizes that in many instances it just isn't happening. The corporate world has experienced the result of what is left untaught and is seeking to make a positive difference. Many companies sponsor mentoring programs, allowing employees to leave work to help at-risk students with their studies. Other corporations and community minded individuals sponsor in-service training for teachers and fund curriculum that teaches the principles they want their future employees/fellow citizens to have. Some companies and individuals —the exceptional ones—do both.

Corporations and individuals partnering with schools to give students what they truly need to make it in life provide a winning combination for everyone. Businesses get employees who have the values of integrity, honesty, and loyalty; schools get students who are cooperative, willing, and excited about getting their education, and the students learn values and skills that will benefit them for the whole of their lives.

In 1992, the principal of Colleyville Middle School, G. Paul Jennings, wanted to recognize Mike Gustin of Colleyville, Texas, as an individual who stepped forward to support educational excellence in his community. In a letter to the Secretary of Education, The Honorable Lamar Alexander, Jennings explained how Mike Gustin, the Chief Executive Officer of Amtrade International, an oil exploration firm with offices worldwide, provided funding in excess of $25,000 to purchase "The I CAN Curriculum" for local schools. In part, here's what Mr. Jennings had to say:

> *From time to time we educators call upon the various business representatives in our communities to assist us with programs and, in many cases, actually fund a "concept" that we feel is integral to the positive growth and development of the nation's youngsters. As you are all too well aware, the nation's middle school population is in need of a "shot in the arm."*
>
> *While it is true that interdisciplinary teaming, cooperative learning, peer tutoring, and many more*

programs designed to promote student advocacy are currently in place in our schools, it has become glaringly evident that the self-image of the average middle school student is in need of daily attention. A local businessman and parent came to me with an exciting idea to assist in boosting the self-images of our youngsters. The integral concept of "The I Can Curriculum" was the development of well-rounded students through a series of motivational activities designed to assist students in setting goals, building positive relationships, learning the importance of honesty, integrity, and loyalty, and building a firm foundation for success in life. Mr. Gustin also furnished all of the teachers with training so that they could work with their students in providing a framework for success in life...I simply wanted you to know that Mr. Gustin is a "Point of Light" in our community and we are definitely proud that he cares enough to make a difference.

The "Point of Light" Mr. Jennings referred to, in case the last decade has dulled your memory, is in reference to the strategy, AMERICA 2000, President George Bush put in place when he became President in 1989. I quote him here, "Our challenge amounts to nothing less than a revolution in American education. A battle for our future. And now, I ask all Americans to be points of light in the crusade that counts the most: The crusade to prepare our children and ourselves for the exciting future that looms ahead. At any moment in every mind, the miracle of learning beckons us all."

Secretary of Education Lamar Alexander was so moved by the letter he received from Principal Jennings that he wrote a personal letter to Mike Gustin. Here is a little of what he had to say,

"...At the heart of our journey to educational excellence are educators, students, families, businesses and communities committed to success. By encouraging outstanding academic performance, community leaders like you are helping bring examples of success to the front of our AMERICA 2000 revolution.

"Americans have always had a special knack for discovery and invention—the word 'impossible' is never associated with an American idea or dream. By emphasizing educational innovation through business cooperation, you represent a return to the 'can do' values that established our nation as a world leader."

Educational innovation is what I am making a point about today. You can be an innovator! You can help your company, your church, your community, see the importance of teaching honesty, integrity, values, loyalty, leadership and the tools necessary for balanced, healthy living to a generation of youth who have done with too little concrete instruction for way too long.

Corporate Sponsorship

Without a doubt, my best example of an individual making a difference in the lives of students is Dr. Angela T. Rasmussen of Tampa, Florida. I was indeed fortunate to spend time with this dynamic woman and her husband, Dr. Rick Rasmussen. It had been her desire to meet her hero, Mr. Zig Ziglar, while she was in his home town of Plano, Texas, participating in the 1992 Mrs. USA National Pageant, but Mr. Ziglar was out of town so I was sent in his stead.

Angela did not win Mrs. USA that weekend but she was thrilled to have been a part of the pageant and even more excited about the platform she had chosen for her year long reign as Mrs. Florida. Her goal was to place "The I CAN Curriculum" in every school in Florida. She strongly believes that many students don't have the luxury of being taught about work ethics, honesty, character and integrity, and that the business community has a responsibility to instill in our youth the foundation and values for a moral and successful life. We visited at length about the best way to approach her task and I tried to explain a little about "edu-crats" and the red tape often associated with implementing new curriculum. I suggested that she begin her efforts in her own community, Hillsborough County, and spread out from there.

Dr. Rasmussen was already a member of the Board of Directors of the Hillsborough Educational Foundation, an organization that strives to enhance educational opportunities for students in Hillsborough County public schools. She contacted the Executive Director of the foundation, Mr. Terry Boehm, and told him of her desire to start an annual golf tournament to raise funds to purchase "The I CAN Curriculum" for Hillsborough County students. The foundation has strongly supported her efforts from the very beginning.

The very first "Project I CAN" golf tournament was held in September of 1992. Angela and her staff at Gentle Dentistry organized the entire event, from the lovely banquet for Corporate Sponsors at Busch Gardens, to obtaining the prizes, trophies and T-shirts that were given away at the tournament. The format for determining which schools would receive the "I CAN" grant money required the school principal to write an essay explaining why his/her school needed the "I CAN" principles taught in their school more than any other school in the district. An appointed committee selected three finalists and the winner was announced at the Sunday night banquet at Busch Gardens.

I went to the winning school on the following Tuesday morning and taught the teachers how to successfully implement the "I CAN Curriculum." They also learned how to give a pre- and a post-course survey, which involved a questionnaire about character traits, and they learned how to measure the results at the end of the year.

I always suggest that the schools agree to and sign a contract before the course is implemented and there were no exceptions in this case. The contract insures that the curriculum is presented in the most effective manner and that the students receive the greatest benefit. Following is an example of what one of the junior high schools agreed to:

The I CAN Contract

(The Grant Sponsor's/Foundation's Name) will provide the following:

1) Additional teacher training

2) One 2 year pre-paid tuition scholarship for a student meeting the following requirements:

   • Eligible for the free and reduced price school meal plan

   • Sign an agreement to stay in school and remain drug and crime free

   • Demonstrate a record of school and community service

   • Demonstrate a special need or special family circumstance

3) New student booklets

(The name of the school) agrees to the following:

   • Develop a written plan for the implementation of the program

   • Designate an on-site coordinator

   • Pre- and post-tests of the entire student population (materials provided by I CAN)

- Provide other evaluation information, such as pre- and post-I CAN:

  GPAs

  Student referrals, suspensions and expulsions

  Teacher conduct grades

  Daily attendance rates

- Provide at least three student nominations for the I CAN scholarships

- Follow implementation instructions completely

- Complete an evaluation report by (date)

- Continue the program for at least two additional years

- Work cooperatively with the (Grant Sponsor/ Foundation) and Alexander Resource Group to ensure the success of the I CAN program.

I have read and fully understand the terms of the I CAN contract.

(Grant/Foundations Director)

(Principal of School)

(School's I CAN Contact Person)

(Contact Person's Signature)

I returned to the winning school in January and again about three months later to ensure that the teachers had implemented the program as instructed.

It has been almost ten years since Dr. Angela Rasmussen and I first discussed her dream of implementing the I CAN program in Florida schools and her enthusiasm for the course continues to grow. In a recent letter she wrote that "one of life's sweetest blessings is when you can set a goal and see it being realized....as is the case with 'Project I CAN.'" She went on to share some of her experiences with the program:

The business community has truly "bought into" investing in our youth. They realize that it is truly a win/win situation. If our kids are exposed to building their lives on a solid moral foundation, if they are shown how to set and achieve goals, if they realize the importance of relationships, they make much better employees or employers! Through job mentoring, job shadowing, in-kind donations, and $300,000 in cash donations, over the past 10 years the business community annually sees their return on their investment at our annual recognition dinner where students from the "I Can" program stand up and witness what "I Can" has meant to them.

*To date 4,000 students have experienced "Project
I Can." We continue to see improved school spirit,
renewed enthusiasm for teaching, and an overall "I
Can" attitude among teachers and students alike.*

*We have established scholarship funds and have
awarded eleven scholarships to date. This enables
these students a full four year scholarship, provided
they stay in school, stay crime free, drug free, and
maintain good grades.*

Angela happily reports that Hillsborough
County and the business community "CAN DO"
what is needed to make I CAN available to the
students in their school district. The figures I used
in Chapter 8 from teacher Charlene Garrett of
Dowdell Junior High School are a direct result of
Dr. Angela Rasmussen's work with the
Hillsborough County School District. If all of
America had more Americans like Angela, our
students would have everything they need to grow
into well balanced, happy adults.

Another individual who has a real heart for
kids is Lloyd Ward, former President of Frito Lay
Central Division. He first contacted me with
questions about I CAN and once I explained the
program, he said he wanted to develop a plan for
getting it into one of the 29 low performing high
schools in the State of Texas that the Texas

Education Commission was going to close if test scores were not improved. A. Maceo Smith High School in Dallas, Texas, was selected and the plan was put into action.

The first step was to have a community meeting. Parents were invited to the school for a program that provided some entertainment as well as an opportunity to explain the program. Promotional materials were designed and sent out to the news media, business leaders, parents and concerned citizens, strongly urging them to attend. Refreshments were served and the school band and chorus performed. Afterwards, Lloyd Ward talked about his company's three-year plan to underwrite the program that they believed would improve the kids' chances of having more opportunities for a successful life.

The second step was convincing the teachers that they really did want to teach yet another curriculum. When they realized our program dealt with the real problems the kids were facing, the environment in which they were living, the fact that many of the kids were literally raising themselves or lived in single parent homes, they got interested. They knew many of their students came from very poor backgrounds and didn't even expect to live to the age of 20. Yet the teachers came to see how affection and direction from them, like goal setting and character training, could help them make a true difference in their students' lives.

The third step was an assembly to explain the program to the 1000 plus student body and to implement the program. It got off to an unusually slow start, as it was hard to convince students with so many outside negative influences that they were, in fact, important people, that they could succeed in life, and that they could be anything in life they wanted to be if they built their life on a solid foundation, acquired a good attitude and self-confidence, and learned how to get along well with other people.

Slowly but surely some positive things began to happen. Another assembly was held and the drama club, band and chorus presented a program based on the I CAN Curriculum; it was magnificent. Shortly after that the kids were invited to perform at a huge seminar in Dallas at Reunion Arena. Nineteen thousand people saw the students from A. Maceo Smith High School perform that day, and 19,000 people gave them a standing ovation when the performance was over—surely an overwhelming moment that will shine brightly in their memories for years to come.

I included the figures for the first year of I CAN implementation at A. Maceo Smith High

School in Chapter 8. They were outstanding - and they are the direct result of the vision of one man, Lloyd Ward of Frito Lay, who took action on that vision and made a huge difference in the lives of hundreds of students.

It is my prayer that you'll consider the influence Mike Gustin, Dr. Angela Rasmussen, and Lloyd Ward, three business people, have had on thousands of our youth, and that you'll begin to consider what you can do to motivate businesses to join you in making a difference in your community today.

Robert Louis Stevenson once said, "The man is a success who has lived well, laughed often and loved much; who has gained the respect of intelligent men and the love of children; who leaves the world better than he found it, whether by an improved poppy, a perfect poem, or a rescued soul; who never lacked appreciation of earth's beauty or failed to express it; who looked for the best in others and gave the best he had." Mike, Angela and Lloyd have done their part. What about you?

chapter ten

Introducing
Your Community
to "The I CAN Program"

The I CAN Program is a philosophy of life that teaches that our greatest achievements are sparked by two powerful words… I CAN. These words inspire our confidence, serve as testament to our determination to succeed, and reflect a desire to be our very best. This is the reason that thousands of educators, students, and parents across America are excited about the program. As previously mentioned, it is based on the foundational principles of honesty, integrity, character, trust, loyalty and love—principles upon which successful lives are built. Once this solid foundation is established, individuals develop a positive attitude and self-image, as well as strong, healthy relationships with others. Even more importantly, they are empowered to achieve their life's goals and desires. Health, happiness, prosperity, friendship, peace and security are dreams transformed into everyday realities. I believe this is what we all want for our children.

From my perspective, it is important that we teach our children these principles today because these are the principles that will run our businesses and our country tomorrow. The Secretary of Labor and members of the Secretary's Commission on Achieving Necessary Skills (SCANS) reported that more than half of our nation's young people leave school without the knowledge or foundation required to find and hold a good job. This is sobering news for teachers, students, parents and employers. The work force of the 21st Century, the SCANS Report further indicated, will not only need to be creative and responsible problem-solvers, but workers must possess the skills and attitudes on which employers can build.

The I CAN program is committed to developing the positive attitudes that will help young people be successful in their personal and academic endeavors now and professionally in the future. I CAN achieves this by not only motivating the students, but by focusing on the attitudes of those who most influence today's young people —parents and teachers. It's a comprehensive strategy that serves to cement the bond between teachers, students and parents.

Keynote Addresses/In-Service Workshops

Next to parents, teachers are the greatest, most influential role models in the lives of children. Teachers are truly the everyday heroes who can make a difference in the lives of children who can, in turn, grow up to make a difference in America. Yet, with the often overwhelming challenges facing today's educators—drugs, alcohol, violence, teen pregnancy, funding cuts and lack of parental involvement—teachers can become discouraged.

I CAN not only renews educators' hope, it provides them with solutions for coping with "at risk" students. When I am invited into a school or district, I always custom design a teacher in-service agenda to meet the needs of their school's faculty—whether they want a one hour keynote address, a half-day or full day in-service, or a two or three day workshop.

The I CAN in-service/workshop gets participants involved. A study conducted by Stanford University revealed individuals retain 20% of what they hear, 30% of what they see, and 50% of what they see and hear. But retention jumps to a dramatic 85% for individuals who engage in see, hear and do activities. I CAN optimizes educators' in-service experience by involving them in instructional see, hear and do activities that are fun. Participants leave believing in the importance of the I CAN principles. But more importantly, they leave with specific tools that will enable them to make a positive difference in the lives of their students, their school, and their community.

Student Assemblies

One of the most enjoyable events for me personally is when I go to a school to address the students. Why? Because children are the future. Therefore, I believe it is absolutely vital that they see value in themselves, their abilities, and their opportunities for success in life. Children need guidance and a strong helping hand to get them on the right course. Whether it's presented in elementary, middle, or high school assemblies, the I

CAN program nurtures positive self-esteem, attitudes, and behavior in students.

It's a powerful presentation that serves to deter tobacco, drug and alcohol use, dangerous peer pressure, and rebellion against parents and educators. Without question, it's one of the most important assemblies students will ever attend. I also enjoy doing a "Leadership Workshop" with students who are officers in school sponsored clubs. This gives them a wonderful opportunity to learn specific qualities that will enhance their chances of being successful leaders not only while in school, but most importantly, when they graduate.

National I CAN Workshop

In addition to visiting schools individually, we present two powerful days of learning at the National I CAN Workshop held every July in Macon, Georgia. It is a course filled with captivating lectures, exciting discussion, instrumentation, and structured experiences. It's perfect for administrators, counselors, teachers, supervisors, school board members, PTA/PTO members, and parents. With the nationally known speakers that present every year, it is guaranteed to be one of the most powerful educational workshops in America. You won't want to miss it. It will change your life...as an educator...as a parent...as an individual.

The I CAN Character Curriculum

One of the most important facets of the I CAN Program is the I CAN Curriculum. There are two complete curriculums—the beginner program for children in kindergarten through 5th grade, and the achiever program for those in 6th grade and above. Thousands of public and private schools across America are currently teaching the I CAN Course—touching millions of children's lives. Educators are discovering that teaching the program just 15 minutes a week really creates a positive change in student behavior. The course helps uncover the root causes of bad habits and attitudes and successfully replaces them with the positive attitudes that enable students to enjoy positive relationships with their parents, teachers, and classmates.

How to Get Started

Each year we send out thousands of brochures to schools all across America regarding the I CAN Program. This includes information on all of the above facets of the program. Superintendents, staff development coordinators, curriculum directors, principals and counselors are generally the ones to whom we send information. These leaders can contact our company and we will schedule an in-service program for the teachers or students to address their needs. If they are interested in the I CAN course, we simply answer any questions about its content or implementation and immediately ship the program to them. We always make recommendations on their needs and budget. If the budget allows, we recommend that every teacher in the school have his own curriculum. This way allows them to write notes, examples, stories, etc., of their own and it becomes customized to their own classroom. If the budget doesn't allow, then we recommend at least one teacher on each grade level have a curriculum, and if the budget still doesn't allow this, then we suggest that at least one teacher in the school teach the program. Many counselors want to take on this responsibility. When multiple curriculums are purchased, we always recommend bringing me in to instruct the teachers on how to implement the program for the most effective results. This also serves as a means by which to renew their commitment to teaching. If the schedule permits, I also like to address the students while I am there, and during certain times of the school year I recommend that they have an evening town hall meeting for parents and business leaders.

The Town Hall Meeting

One of the most direct ways to introduce the I CAN Program to a community is to hold a Town Hall Meeting. This is where the school system invites the entire community to come hear an hour long presentation on the importance of teaching the I CAN Curriculum in their schools and community. I suggest that they publicize the event as much as possible. Letters should be sent home by the school to the parents. Schools should also send letters to the local businesses in town. The letter should basically tell the business leaders how much they have appreciated their time, effort, and financial support of the school in the past, and that the school would like to, in some small way, return the favor by inviting them and all of their employees to a one hour motivational and inspirational session. This actually would serve as a free training session for the employees of their businesses, as well as expose them to the principles that are about to be taught to their children. Many business leaders will, in fact, make a financial contribution to purchasing more of the I CAN Curriculums to be used by the teachers. This is where the schools, parents, and business leaders all come together for the good of surrounding their children with the foundational qualities taught in the I CAN Program. It starts with a step-by-step formula for more effective schools, better educated students, stronger families, and better businesses as a result of having better employees and a stronger, healthier community.

I like to inspire my audience to see the possibilities of having a better community by teaching their youth a solid foundation for living life well through the I CAN philosophy. I explain that the course breathes new life into tired and frustrated teachers. I talk about students seeing the connection between choices and results for the first time and coming to understand that they are the ones making the choices and they can choose to change for the better.

I am always heartened when I conduct a Town Hall Meeting to see how many people have a true concern for the quality of education our youth are receiving today. The meetings are promoted in the newspaper, over the radio, and by announcements sent home from school to parents. Some meetings are held in the Community Center, while others are held at the local high school. They are most effective when teachers, parents, students and community leaders attend.

Building Lehigh Acres Schools Today, a division of Lehigh Acres Community Council, and the Lehigh Acres Educational Task Force sponsored a Town Hall Meeting because they believed "positive self-esteem and the ability to integrate 'character education' into the core curriculum of our schools will promote the welfare of our youth to become 'Leaders of Tomorrow Learning Today.'" Several corporations and individuals supported the program.

One person on fire, like Dr. Angela Rasmussen, can start the whole ball rolling. Calls to local businesses, letters sent to the people who are already supporting the schools at every turn, whether it be by attending all of the sporting events or by assisting teachers in the resource room, get people to the meeting.

Individuals love being singled out as people who have given a lot of time, effort, and even financial support to their local schools. When they receive a letter explaining that the Town Hall Meeting is designed to give something back to them, stating that their name was given as someone who deserved to be recognized and rewarded for their efforts, they will be thrilled.

They are informed of the very inspirational, exciting, motivational and fun one hour presentation that I'll deliver and are invited to bring their employees and their kids as guests. What the meeting says to those individuals is that, even though it doesn't happen very often, they are being told how much they are appreciated.

After they've heard the presentation, they can choose to help by seeing that their schools teach the I CAN concepts and principles or they can wait and spend twenty-five times as much money to train their workers when they enter the work force. Now, it doesn't take a rocket scientist or a Phi Beta Kappa to figure out the right answer to the question, "When do I first start encouraging my future employees to feel good about themselves?"

If they have seen the logic of teaching character, integrity, responsibility, honesty, and the other character traits that lead to good citizenship, they will want to know how to help their school district implement a curriculum that will teach kids the principles they want them to have. In fact, at this point they have a desire to be business partners in excellence with their school system.

The I CAN Mayor!

When Rudy Giuliani first became Mayor of New York City, the problems were so huge most of its citizens believed the city was actually unmanageable. Times Square was an immoral sewer and it wasn't safe to go in many parts of the city after dark. Giuliani did not believe New York City was unmanageable, and he charted a course to change things. He started with basics and fundamentals. He resolved that graffiti would be removed from the subway trains. He recognized that appearances make a difference. He also cracked down on people who ran through or around subway turnstiles to avoid paying. Then, the dreaded 'squeegee' thugs (street vandals who washed car windows at stoplights intimidating the drivers for cash donations) were rounded up and eliminated. The result of these small beginnings put New York City on a new course and today the city is one of the safest in America.

There are two points I want to make with this story. The first point is that one person with a vision can make a difference. The next point is that when you begin to do some simple basic things that are right and correct, they will lay a solid foundation for a huge change. The same can be said for the power of character-based education. The simple thing we must do as educators is teach our young people the three principles I established at the beginning of this book: Honesty, Accepting Responsibility, and Respect for Others. The I CAN Program is a perfect tool to achieve this objective. All your school needs to get started is a person with a vision. Can you be the Rudy Giuliani in your community? I think the answer is obvious. YES—YOU CAN!

Conclusion

The events of September 11, 2001, have changed America in many ways. We (Americans) have been rudely awakened and are looking for things that have meaning and value. We have new ideas about family and the things that are really important. What must be foremost in our minds and hearts are the future generations of Americans who must be prepared to meet the challenges of a world that is changing before our eyes each day. To meet the challenges of the future, our national character must be strong and we must have the will to persevere and stay on a course that will secure our future and sustain our freedom.

The challenges of meeting the needs of future generations rest primarily in the hands of parents and teachers. Government programs and politicians can provide funding for some important things, but the real solutions will be found in the hearts and minds of those who are closest to our children. As an educator, you are one of those people. I hope this little book has helped create a vision for you and for your students. I hope you agree that the issues of Honesty, Accepting Responsibility, and Respect for Others are fundamental qualities that will help prepare our young people for life. More importantly, I hope you will be willing to become a difference maker in your school and in your community.

The I CAN Curriculum

*Two powerful words that inspire
our confidence...Serve as a testament to our
determination to succeed... And reflect
a desire to be our very best.*

That's why thousands of educators, students and parents across America are excited about the I CAN program. Through I CAN, they're not only learning the ABCs of education, but more importantly, the ABCs of Life—Attitude, Behavior, and Character. These are the fundamentals that enable individuals to achieve their fullest potential and bring out the best in others.

The I CAN program is based on the foundational principles of honesty, integrity, character, trust, loyalty and love—principles upon which successful lives are built. Once this solid foundation is established, individuals develop a positive attitude and self-image, as well as strong, healthy relationships with others. Even more importantly, they are empowered to achieve their life's goals and desires. Health, happiness, prosperity, friendship, peace and security are dreams transformed into everyday realities. Isn't that what we all want? Especially for today's youth?

The I CAN program is committed to developing the positive attitudes which will help our nation's young people be successful in their personal and academic endeavors now and professionally in the future.

The I CAN Beginner's Curriculum (Grades K-5)

A flexible, easy-to-use format, innovative ideas and posi-tive motivational themes combine to make the I CAN curriculum a welcome asset to any classroom. The cur-riculum contains many options for adaptation, allowing for modification as needed.

The I CAN Achiever Curriculum (Grades 6-12)

Like the K-5 curriculum, this program is an effective "hands on" tool to help students help themselves. This dynamic curriculum is designed to take the teacher through the entire six segments with extensive teacher's notes, tips, procedures to follow, bonus section and more.

The I CAN Student Workbook (Grades 6-12)

(Achiever Only)

What qualities define a leader? How do individuals gain positions of leadership? The former Director of Educational Services and Director of Sales for the Zig Ziglar Corporation has worked with scores of business and education leaders over the years.

Making It Happen provides a simple, practical solution to some serious challenges faced by leaders on a daily basis in all walks of life.

Alexander believes that leaders cannot expect results from others if they are unwilling to produce results themselves. Leaders must set an example for others and maintain a critical matrix of leadership tools. *Making It Happen* highlights these two requirements for leadership success and provides readers with a roadmap for achievement.

Executives and managers who want to improve their organizations' ability to work together and be more productive will find solutions in Alexander's book. He recognizes the special niche held by operational managers who must lead, manage and inspire daily performance and accomplishment in others.

To order **Making It Happen**, call 1-478-476-9081 or order online at www.yesican.net

A C.H.A.R.T. for Leadership

What personal qualities do leaders need to be successful? What impact does good leadership have in the workplace? In this fast-paced program, Bob explains the qualities shared by successful leaders, and teaches you how to use them to create a value system shared by 91% of the Fortune 500 CEOs.

An Evening of Inspiration

In our hurry up, get-it-done-yesterday society, we often find ourselves "stretched" and "stressed" in many directions. In this educational, inspirational and humorous tape, Bob teaches us how three biblical characteristics can make your personal, family and business life come together smoothly.

To order these cassettes, call 1-478-476-9081
or order online at www.yesican.net

Conference and Speaking Engagements

Whether you are looking for a motivational, inspirational, or humorous keynote address by a nationally known speaker, or a sales trainer and business consultant to teach specific leadership, management, customer service, or sales skills, Bob will exceed your expectations.

If you are interested in having Bob Alexander speak at your upcoming event or would like a list of current prices for The I CAN curriculum, books, or cassettes, contact:

The Alexander Resource Group

176 Lake View Dr. North
Macon, GA 31210
Phone/Fax: (478) 476-9081
Email: bob@yesican.net
website: www.yesican.net

As **Bob Alexander** finished competing in a national black belt karate tournament and within the same week completed his eighteenth marathon in New York City, he said, "I'm tired." While this is not a particularly startling comment, just reading his accomplishments fatigues most people. Bob has excelled in almost every aspect of his life. As an outstanding high school student who consistently won honors, Bob carried that tradition into his college career where he excelled as a dean's list student, karate instructor and brigade commander in ROTC.

Bob's desire to help other people led him into the field of education. He was a winning teacher, coach, and high school administrator who learned from experience the challenges students and teachers face. He was selected as "Outstanding Young Man in America" in recognition of his professional achievements and his superior leadership ability combined with exceptional service to his community.

To fulfill his goals for personal growth, Bob left education to take on the challenge of sales. His outstanding sales and leadership ability helped him rapidly climb the corporate ladder and become vice president of sales for the company's North American operation.

Zig Ziglar invited Bob to join his team in 1988 because Bob is a proven leader. In 1990 he was promoted to general sales manager and in 1992 became the Director of Educational Services. Today, as president of The Alexander Resource Group, he continues traveling the country sharing his proven plan of prosperity which has helped thousands of students, teachers, school administrators, salespeople, managers, and business executives improve their attitudes, develop self-confidence, set specific goals and live their dreams.